Illness Politics and Hashtag Activism

Forerunners: Ideas First

Short books of thought-in-process scholarship, where intense analysis, questioning, and speculation take the lead

FROM THE UNIVERSITY OF MINNESOTA PRESS

(Continued on page 121)

Illness Politics and Hashtag Activism

Lisa Diedrich

University of Minnesota Press

MINNEAPOLIS

LONDON

A previous version of chapter 2 appeared as "Weaponizing Weakness, Diagnosing by Gif," on *Nursing Clio,* August 12, 2020, nursingclio.org, CC-BY-NC-SA. A previous version of chapter 5 appeared as "Illness (In) action: CFS and #TimeForUnrest," in *Literature and Medicine* 39, no. 1 (Spring 2021): 8–14; copyright Johns Hopkins University Press.

ISBN 978-1-5179-1734-0 (PB)
ISBN 978-1-4529-7122-3 (Ebook)
ISBN 978-1-4529-7163-6 (Manifold)

Published by the University of Minnesota Press, 2024
111 Third Avenue South, Suite 290
Minneapolis, MN 55401–2520
www.upress.umn.edu

Available as a Manifold edition at manifold.umn.edu

The University of Minnesota is an equal-opportunity educator and employer.

The revolution is here. One podcast, one transcript, one tweet at a time.

—ALICE WONG

Contents

Introduction: #IllnessPolitics

THIS BOOK EXPLORES illness and disability in action on social media, analyzing several popular hashtags as examples of how illness figures, conceptually and strategically, in recent U.S. politics. I demonstrate how illness politics (or #IllnessPolitics, as I have used the term on social media) is informed by, intersects with, and sometimes stands in for, sexual, racial, and class politics. This project is connected to a growing body of work that explores forms of health activism and disability and illness politics as central, not peripheral, to both mainstream and radical politics,[1] as well as work on the dynamic intersection of media and health and health activist

1. On illness and disability politics, see, for example, Eli Clare, *Brilliant Imperfection: Grappling with Care* (Durham, N.C.: Duke University Press, 2017); Johanna Hedva, "Sick Woman Theory," *Mask Magazine* (January 19, 2016); Shayda Kafai, *Crip Kinship: The Disability Justice and Art Activism of Sins Invalid* (Vancouver: Arsenal Pulp Press, 2021); Alison Kafer, *Feminist, Queer, Crip* (Bloomington: Indiana University Press, 2013); Akemi Nishida, *Just Care: Messy Entanglements of Disability, Dependency, and Desire* (Philadelphia: Temple University Press, 2022); Leah Lakshmi Piepzna-Samarasinha, *Care Work: Dreaming Disability Justice* (Vancouver: Arsenal Pulp Press, 2018); Jasbir Puar, *The Right to Maim: Debility, Capacity, Disability* (Durham, N.C.: Duke University Press, 2017); Ellen Samuels, *Fantasies of Identification: Disability, Gender, Race* (New York: NYU Press, 2014); Sami Schalk, *Black Disability Politics* (Durham, N.C.: Duke University Press, 2022); and Alice Wong, ed., *Disability Visibility First-Person Stories from the Twenty-first Century* (New York: Vintage, 2020).

practices.[2] Illness- and disability-oriented hashtags serve as portals into how and why illness and disability are sites of political struggle.

I first take up two hashtags—#SickHillary and #TrumpIsNotWell—used in the U.S. presidential election campaigns of 2016 and 2020, respectively, to demonstrate how illness politics has operated in recent mainstream electoral politics where illness functions as a metaphor for a candidate's supposed unfitness for office. I then explore illness and disability activist hashtags—#ADAPTandRESIST, #CripTheVote, and #TimeForUnrest—as examples of counterportals into other forms of illness-thought-activism in time.[3] My last chapter on #LongCOVID doesn't conclude so much as foreground the ongoingness of illness politics as an enduring struggle against ableism and stigma and for care, access, and full citizenship and personhood.

2. On the visual culture of health and medicine, see, for example, Olivia Banner, *Communicative Biocapitalism: The Voice of the Patient in Digital Health and the Health Humanities* (Ann Arbor: University of Michigan Press, 2017); Lisa Cartwright, *Screening the Body: Tracing Medicine's Visual Culture* (Minneapolis: University of Minnesota Press, 1995); Lester Friedman and Theresa Jones, eds., *Routledge Handbook of Health and Media* (New York: Routledge, 2022); Emma Bedor Hiland, *Therapy Tech: The Digital Transformation of Mental Healthcare* (Minneapolis: University of Minnesota Press 2021); Kirsten Ostherr, *Medical Visions: Producing the Patient through Film, Television, and Imagining Technologies* (New York: Oxford University Press, 2013); Clive Seale, *Media and Health* (London: Sage, 2002); and David Serlin, *Imagining Illness: Public Health and Visual Culture* (Minneapolis: University of Minnesota Press, 2010). On media and health activism, see Gregg Bordowitz, *The AIDS Crisis Is Ridiculous and Other Writings, 1986–2003* (Cambridge, Mass.: MIT Press, 2006); and Marika Cifor, *Viral Cultures: Activist Archiving in the Age of AIDS* (Minneapolis: University of Minnesota Press, 2022).

3. There are many hashtags connected to, or variations on, the hashtags I discuss here—for example, #HillarysHealth, #SummerOfADAPT, and #MillionsMissing. There are also many, many other hashtags that have generated disability and illness politics in the last several years—#SaveMedicaid, #SaveTheADA, #IAmAPreexistingCondition, #AbleismExists, #DisabilitySolidarity, #DeafInPrison, #AccessIsLove, to name just a few.

My work centers illness as a category of analysis. In my first book, *Treatments,* I investigated the ways that illness narratives can be read as symptomatic texts of our time in two respects: as texts that literally describe symptoms (and struggle with finding a form to describe the affective and physical experience of symptoms) and as texts that describe illness as an event that goes beyond any individual's experience and account of it, reflecting wider cultural categories including race, gender, class, and sexuality. At the center of *Treatments* is the figure of the politicized patient and the practice of illness politics. I locate the emergence of this figure around 1980 and discuss Sontag's *Illness as Metaphor* (1978) and Audre Lorde's *The Cancer Journals* (1980) as hinge texts between the women's health movement of the 1970s and AIDS activism of the 1980s.

I ended *Treatments* with what I called an "ethics of failure" because I wanted to make a case for the ubiquity and importance of failure in our scientific, political, and artistic practices and to explore how our subjectivities, research methods, and objects of study are constituted by our failures as much as by our successes. In my formulation of this ethical practice, failure becomes not an ending but a beginning of other ways of seeing and being in the world. My second book, *Indirect Action,* ends in a different, if related, register with a discussion of what is most often taken as an image of success, ACT UP's phrase and campaign Drugs into Bodies, a slogan and struggle that transformed the experience and event of AIDS and other illnesses in very concrete, material ways. As I argued in *Indirect Action,* Drugs into Bodies is a complex and ambivalent remainder of the radical success of treatment activism. In a moment in which drugs are delivered as the sole therapeutic solution to all problems—medical, psychological, and social (drugs have even become the solution to drug problems)—the phrase and practice encapsulates a very particular conjuncture of illness-thought-activism in neoliberal times. We are now living the side effects of the success of treatment activism that called for Drugs into Bodies. I wondered: Could it have been and be otherwise?

In thinking about how a phrase like Drugs into Bodies encapsulates a conjuncture of illness-thought-activism in a particular time and place, I realized that hashtags on social media operate in a similar way in the present moment: Drugs into Bodies becomes #DrugsIntoBodies. Hashtags allow for both the condensation and extension of politics in action. In this project, the hashtag-as-portal also serves as a method for analyzing illness politics today. #SickHillary and #TrumpIsNotWell are portals into how Hillary Clinton in 2016 and Donald Trump in 2020 were alleged to be unfit for the presidency, and thus the focus is on the individual political actors named in the hashtags (that Hillary Clinton is always "Hillary" and Donald Trump always "Trump" in these hashtags also indicates the sexual politics at work in mainstream American politics).

Other hashtags point to current counternarratives of illness and disability in action, and in the rest of the chapters I take up recent examples of what we might call, following anthropologist Elizabeth Povinelli, "alternative social projects" to the neoliberalization of healthcare and the relentless ableism of public life.[4] These alternative social projects are all represented by hashtags on social media, and thus the hashtags themselves function to both encapsulate and further multiply and expand the spaces and temporalities of illness and disability in action. The three activist hashtags I discuss—#ADAPTandRESIST, #CripTheVote, and #TimeForUnrest—provide passageways into a multiplicity of forms of illness and disability in action at this time. The hashtags allow people to find an action in a particular moment, but they also operate the other way, extending the action—and thus creating new instantiations of the action in time and space. In her rich portrait of the disability justice performance project Sins Invalid, Shayda Kafai uses Mia Mingus's concept and practice of "leaving evidence"

    4. Elizaabeth A. Povinelli, *Economies of Abandonment: Social Belonging and Endurance in Late Liberalism* (Durham, N.C.: Duke University Press, 2011), 30.

to describe how Sins Invalid's work "leaves evidence so that others in search of community and homecoming can find their way."[5] I argue that hashtags are also a way of leaving evidence, as Mingus herself understands, having started the #AccessIsLove hashtag in collaboration with Alice Wong and the Disability Visibility Project.

As Jackson, Bailey, and Welles note in their book *#Hashtag Activism,* "digital activism is sometimes considered less valid than direct action and is mistakenly regarded as in competition with it."[6] One example of such an argument is Malcolm Gladwell's piece "Small Change" published in *The New Yorker* in 2010. In his usual habit of making big claims based on rather flimsy research, Gladwell argues that the key to effective activism is "strong ties" with "critical friends."[7] He takes the lunch counter sit-ins that began in Greensboro, North Carolina, in 1960 as his example of how activism emerges, spreads, and brings about change. He notes a change from the 1960s to the present, claiming, "Where activists were once defined by their causes, they are now defined by their tools."[8] This is a huge generalization, of course, that fails to understand that Civil Rights activists in the 1960s also used tools and had media and communications strategies. It also relies on a very

5. Kafai, *Crip Kinship,* 93. Kafai cites Mia Mingus's *Leaving Evidence* blog, which asserts on its opening page, "We must leave evidence. Evidence that we were here, that we existed, that we survived and love and ached," https://leavingevidence.wordpress.com. See also the conversation between Mingus and Alice Wong on leaving evidence that Kafai also cites, *"Disability Visibility Project:* Mia Mingus, Part 3," August 23, 2014, https://disabilityvisibilityproject.com/2014/09/27/disability-visibility-project-mia-mingus-alice-wong-3/.

6. Sarah J. Jackson, Moya Bailey, and Brooke Foucault Welles, *#Hashtag Activism: Networks of Race and Gender Justice* (Cambridge, Mass.: MIT Press, 2020), xxxii.

7. Malcolm Gladwell, "Small Change: Why the Revolution Will Not Be Tweeted," *The New Yorker,* September 27, 2010, https://www.newyorker.com/magazine/2010/10/04/small-change-malcolm-gladwell.

8. Gladwell.

ableist attitude about what activism looks like.[9] As Jackson, Bailey, and Welles argue, hashtags can be a conduit for social change, especially because they provide a mechanism for generating interest in activism and connections between activists. Neither Gladwell nor Jackson, Bailey, and Welles mention illness or disability activism on social media. Thus, *Illness Politics and Hashtag Activism* adds to the literature on social media and activism by critiquing the ableism of dominant images of activism. This critique shows that disabled and chronically ill people who may be limited in their capacity to move freely and tirelessly through the world can still do politics and be activists. Indeed, online spaces create connections among sick and disabled people and allow for greater participation in social and political life. Or, as Kafai puts it in a chapter on Sins Invalid's practice of "Crip Kinship and Cyber Love" through regular conversations and events available through Facebook and on their website and YouTube channel, "There is radical possibility in this broadening of space and crip home, in understanding that crip-centric liberated zones can be intentionally created anywhere."[10]

I locate this project in the most general sense at the intersection of the interdisciplinary fields of critical health studies, disability studies, and digital humanities. More specifically, the project draws on recent work in disability studies that looks at the ableism in contemporary political cultures and activist movements. An early

---

9. Gladwell really shows his cards at the end of "Small Change," when he sets up what we might call a straw-activist as a contrast to those who risked their lives to participate in the sit-ins and voter-registration campaigns in the South in the 1960s. Gladwell discusses a story in Clay Shirky's *Here Comes Everybody: The Power of Organizing without Organizations* (New York: Penguin, 2009), in which someone working on Wall Street uses social media to recover their phone that had been found/stolen by a teenage girl. Gladwell portentously writes that Shirky "portentously" asks "What happens next?" And he ends his essay with this glib answer: "What happens next is more of the same. A networked, weak-tie world is good at things like helping Wall Streeters get phones back from teen-age girls. *Viva la revolución.*"

10. Kafai, *Crip Kinship*, 126.

influential piece is Johanna Hedva's essay "Sick Woman Theory" from 2016, which begins with an image of Hedva in bed listening to a Black Lives Matters protest near her house in Los Angeles in 2014: "Attached to my bed, I rose up my sick woman fist, in solidarity."[11] Hedva discusses Hannah Arendt's formulation of the political as requiring a person's presence in public, noting that such a definition means "whole swathes of the population can be deemed *a*-political—simply because they are not physically able to get their bodies into the street."[12] Following Judith Butler's work on vulnerability and resistance, which I will also draw on in chapter 5, Hedva proposes "Sick Woman Theory" as an articulation of an anticapitalist form of protest that begins with and enacts care for oneself and others.[13]

In the preface to their collection of essays *Care Work: Dreaming Disability Justice*, Leah Lakshmi Piepzna-Samarasinha provides another counterimage to ableism, as summarized in the preface's title: "Writing (with) a Movement from Bed."[14] In theories and practices of disability justice, the bed, according to Piepzna-Samarasinha, is a site not only of rest and containment but of creativity and activism, and dreaming becomes both a personal and collective experience.[15]

11. Hedva, "Sick Woman Theory." Hedva's essay can still be found circulating online, although the original link at maskmagazine.com is no longer available.

12. Hedva, "Sick Woman Theory"; Hannah Arendt, *The Human Condition* (Chicago: University of Chicago Press, 1958).

13. Hedva, "Sick Woman Theory"; Judith Butler, *Notes toward a Performative Theory of Assembly* (Cambridge, Mass.: Harvard University Press, 2015).

14. Piepzna-Samarasinha, *Care Work*.

15. In 2021, Patrisia Macías-Rojas, along with Akemi Nishida and Ronak Kapadia, organized a series of Zoom conversations on the topic of "The Reciprocal Politics of Bed Space Activism: From Confinement to Radical Care" as part of the Humanities Without Walls project at the University of Illinois at Chicago Institute for the Humanities. In her introduction to the first conversation and series, Macías-Rojas mentioned AIDS activist and filmmaker Marlon Riggs and disability activist and writer Stacey Park Milbern as activists who did significant work from their beds.

As they explain, "Disability justice allowed me to understand that me writing from my sickbed wasn't me being weak or uncool or not a real writer but a time-honored crip creative practice."[16] Along with, or emerging from, the sickbed, Piepzna-Samarasinha documents the multiple sites of disability justice in action, including online and social media sites:

> Much of our coming together has been through zines, online disabled QT/POC communities, Tumblr and blog and social media posts, or through three people getting together at a kitchen table or a group Skype call to start to hesitantly talk about our lives, organize a meal train, share pills and tips, or post the thoughts about activism and survival we have at two in the morning. It is underdocumented, private work—work often seen as not "real activism." But it is the realest activism there is. This is how disability justice art and activism change the world and save lives.[17]

Part of this practice of documenting the underdocumented is making connections with disabled artist-activists across space and time. In their essay "So Much Time Spent in Bed: A Letter to Gloria Anzaldúa on Chronic Illness, Coatlicue, and Creativity," Piepzna-Samarasinha describes the bed as "the nepantla place of opening."[18] They conjure meeting Anzaldúa in an intimate encounter "in the chronically ill sickbed heaped with pillows where

---

See also Nishida, *Just Care,* which includes a chapter on bed activism that draws on work by Hedva, Piepzna-Samarasinha, and Gloria Anzaldúa, among others, to explore "not only conventional activism that disabled and sick people engage in from their beds (e.g., joining protests via the internet), but also bed-born wisdom and dreams emerging in the middle of bed dwellers' moments of enduring pain, fatigue, depression, and other bodymind conditions," 39.

16. Piepzna-Samarasinha, *Care Work,* 17.

17. Piepzna-Samarasinha, 19.

18. Piepzna-Samarasinha, 181. For a discussion of Anzaldúa's work as an expression of sickness and pain, see Suzanne Bost, *Incarnación: Illness and Body Politics in Chicana Feminist Literature* (New York: Fordham University Press, 2009).

we both spend so much time."[19] In this "sexy" image, writing in bed creates access to a dream time that is based on reciprocity and interdependence. The question of what "real activism" is and looks like in practice, and where it happens, is important to this project and all my work. How we do illness and disability and/as politics is not one thing, and the hashtags I discuss in this book show this multiplicity in action.

Along with recent work in disability studies and documenting disability justice in action, *Illness Politics and Hashtag Activism* also connects to recent work on digital health humanities and the relationship between health and media, as well as, more generally, analysis that considers practices of political activism on social media.[20] By analyzing the politics of illness and disability on social media, I hope this book will also serve as a resource for assessing and counteracting the ableism that currently infuses politics in the United States and as a guidebook for activists looking for models for doing #IllnessPolitics on social media.

In each chapter, I describe how the projects behind the hashtags emerged and operate on social media and in the wider world before considering what they tell us about the conjuncture of illness-thought-activism in the present. In general, I am interested in the question: Why does illness and disability in action take these forms in this moment? More specifically, I ask: What spaces do different projects occupy and/or attempt to create? What temporalities are

19. Piepzna-Samarasinha, *Care Work,* 182.

20. Along with Jackson, Bailey, and Welles, see also Zeynep Tufekci, *Twitter and Tear Gas: The Power and Fragility of Networked Protest* (New Haven, Conn.: Yale University Press, 2017). In *Viral Cultures,* Marika Cifor discusses the circulation of images of AIDS activism on online platforms like Tumblr. She acknowledges (206) the problem of the commodification, decontextualization, and depoliticization when images of activism circulate, but also argues that GIFs can and have been used as a form of activist illness politics. As one example, she mentions the Undetectable Collective's Tumblr site, which became a space for making and collecting animated GIFs to counteract stigma and generate conversation around HIV/AIDS.

at work in relation to different illnesses and illness politics? What kinds of subjects are produced by various forms of illness and disability politics?

The Chapters: Hashtags as Portals

Each chapter takes a hashtag as a portal through which to view illness and disability politics in action. Although I designate a single hashtag to focus my analysis, I will reference other related hashtags and social media campaigns, reflecting the way hashtags often lead to other hashtags and campaigns in practice on social media. In chapter 1, I discuss the hashtag #SickHillary, which was started by alt-right provocateur Mike Cernovich and used on Twitter, Instagram, and Facebook to cast aspersions on Hillary Clinton's physical and moral health. I introduce the concept and practice of "diagnosing by gif," a phenomenon that first became standard fare on 24–7 cable news channels. On social media the phenomenon is more condensed and concentrated, and images can circulate even more widely. Looping and other visual techniques direct our attention and make visible something we might not otherwise see. One effect of diagnosing by gif is to produce an ableist way of seeing or what Ellen Samuels calls a "fantasy of disability identification," in which "disability is a knowable, obvious, and unchanging category."[21]

In chapter 2, I look at the Lincoln Project's social media campaign organized around the hashtag #TrumpIsNotWell that sought to show Trump was unfit during the presidential campaign of 2020. I connect this campaign with earlier attempts to diagnose Trump as suffering from mental illness, in particular narcissistic personality disorder. I continue my discussion of the phenomenon of diagnosing by gif, analyzing the digital visual practice as a form of doctoring— meaning "to alter deceptively"—because it takes a moment out of context that focuses the viewer's attention on a purported sign that is then claimed to be symptomatic of a personal problem.

21. Samuels, *Fantasies of Identification,* 121.

After discussing how #IllnessPolitics was used to undermine in very personal, individualized ways the presidential candidacies of both Hillary Clinton and Donald Trump, I turn to several activist hashtags beginning in chapter 3 with the #ADAPTandRESIST campaign, which provides a link to a longer history of disability activism beginning in the 1970s and continuing today. The hashtag was created in 2017 by ADAPT, a disability rights organization with a long history of direct-action politics, to get the message out on social media about a series of actions as a coordinated response to the Trump administration's many policies that increased the vulnerability of disabled people and threatened their access to public space and capacity to live independently.

In chapter 4, I take up #CripTheVote, a hashtag and organization that began before the 2016 election and sought to center disability as a topic of political concern and conversation and increase the political participation of disabled people during the election and after. #CripTheVote's main tactic was to use Twitter chats to generate discussion and awareness for voters and candidates alike about why including a disability perspective was so essential for creating a more inclusive and just society. The increase in conversations explicitly about disability in the 2020 campaign, and the participation of candidates for the Democratic nomination in #CripTheVote Twitter chats, shows the incredible influence #CripTheVote has had through its modes of hashtag activism.

In chapter 5, I continue to explore hashtag activism as a means of political participation for sick and disabled people. In my final case study, I focus on Jennifer Brea's documentary film *Unrest* and the related hashtag #TimeForUnrest. I argue that the film and hashtag work together to connect people with myalgic encephalomyelitis or chronic fatigue syndrome (ME/CFS) and to politicize an illness that is not well understood or treated, and which doctors have often dismissed as psychosomatic. Brea's film has generated attention for ME/CFS and pushed for research into the causes of and treatments for the condition that impacts millions of people (predominantly women) worldwide. With the arrival of the Covid-19 pandemic in

2020 and the emergence of a condition that online patient support groups would name "long Covid," there has been an increased interest in, and some funding for studying, postviral conditions, including ME/CFS. Yet, even as long Covid brings greater attention to chronic postviral conditions, we also see the ongoing struggle in getting doctors and researchers to take seriously conditions that are not well understood. Thus, I end with an illness that for some is unending: in my conclusion, I discuss #LongCOVID and the experience of the ongoingness of illness and illness politics.

1. #SickHillary

ILLNESS IS A key, if undertheorized, aspect of how we do politics now. We saw illness politics at work throughout the long and grueling 2016 presidential campaign. I first became interested in how illness politics circulated on social media with the many stories about Hillary Clinton's health (#HillarysHealth and #SickHillary on social media, to name just two hashtags driving the circulation of stories)—rampant speculation, mainly among those already not supporting her, that she was hiding a secret illness (Parkinson's, traumatic brain injury, epilepsy all circulated as possible diagnoses), which, if revealed, so the story went, would make most Americans realize she was not qualified to be president. In this chapter, I explore some of the illness narratives and politics surrounding Hillary Clinton that began even before she officially announced her second run for the presidency. Along with the scandal surrounding her handling of emails while she was secretary of state, which dominated media coverage of Clinton as a candidate for president in 2016, her health was another key story pushed by right-wing media and Trump himself and further amplified by mainstream media. This can be seen, for example, in the results from a Gallup Daily Tracking poll for the period July 17 to September 18, 2016, asking Americans, "what specifically do you recall reading, hearing or seeing about Hillary Clinton in the last day or two?," results which were used to generate a word map. On the word map, the word *email* is massive, out of proportion with every other word, but *health* is in the next tier of most-mentioned topics.[1] Yet, it is also important to keep in mind, as I will show below, Clinton's emails and Clinton's health were not mutually exclusive topics: emails were released by WikiLeaks that were framed as providing insight into her health problems, a process that linked emails and health as a problem for Clinton in the minds of voters. The constant release of hacked emails, first from the Democratic National Committee and later from John Podesta (Clinton's campaign manager), beginning right before the Democratic National Convention in July, helped make stick the narrative that Clinton had something to hide. So much so that I would argue *email, health, lie,* and *scandal* were connected through a Republican strategy of illness politics.

On Twitter, the hashtag #SickHillary purportedly provided ample evidence that Clinton was not well, feeble even, requiring help getting in and out of cars, walking up steps, needing someone always by her side should she fall or find herself unable to speak. In an article in *The New Yorker* in October 2016, Andrew Marantz introduced Mike Cernovich as the "meme mastermind of the alt-right."[2] In his profile, Marantz discusses how Cernovich first used the phrase "sick Hillary" in a video he made on Periscope the day before Clinton gave a speech in Reno, Nevada, in August 2016 explicitly linking

1. Frank Newport et al., "'Email' Dominates What Americans Have Heard about Clinton," Gallup.com, September 19, 2016, https://news.gallup .com/poll/195596/email-dominates-americans-heard-clinton.aspx. In their coverage of the coverage of the Clinton and Trump campaigns, Newport et al. note that, "Though Clinton has attacked Trump on several issues related to his character, no specific words representing negative traits have 'stuck' to Trump the way the word 'email' has to Clinton." It's fascinating that in this coverage of the coverage of the candidates at this stage of the campaign, no mention is made of the WikiLeaks release of emails. It is highly likely that the curated sharing of specific emails from the Democratic National Convention trove also increased the dominance and stickiness of the word *email* to Clinton.

2. Andrew Marantz, "Trolls for Trump," *The New Yorker,* October 24, 2016, https://www.newyorker.com/magazine/2016/10/31/trolls-for-trump.

Donald Trump to the alt-right and white supremacy. The timing is important. #SickHillary is used to counter Clinton's serious message about Donald Trump and white supremacy. Marantz explained that, for Cernovich, "The word 'sick' described Clinton morally and physically: Cernovich was among the first to insinuate publicly that Clinton had a grave neurological condition, and that the media was covering it up."[3] Marantz also identifies that Cernovich's method of fighting back against "sick Hillary and the #ClintonNewsNetwork" (a dig at the supposed liberal bias of CNN, of course) was by tweeting. According to Marantz, "Internet activism is sometimes derided as 'slacktivism'—a fair characterization when an online campaign tries to, say, cure aids or end child labor. When the goal is to seed social media with misinformation, though, online organizing can be shockingly effective."[4] What is fascinating to me about Marantz's brief reference to various forms of activism is that his assessment relies on, even if not explicitly articulated, a singular image of the activist, who is in the streets and not on Twitter fighting for a better world without AIDS and child labor. Nonetheless, as Marantz recognizes, misinformation is an effective political tactic, and I would add, especially so for the circulation of a kind of illness politics that works through stigma and ableism, as the misinformation circulated through the #SickHillary hashtag shows. We might even say misinformation in this example is a sick tactic in both its form and content.

As Cernovich and others trolled and memed, Clinton's alleged physical illness became an outward sign of her moral depravity—#SickHillary revealed #CrookedHillary. Following Clinton's "coughing fit" while campaigning in Ohio over Labor Day weekend in 2016, right-wing media outlet *Breitbart News* called Clinton a "Choke Artist," going for a triple entendre suggesting illness politics, sexual politics, and electoral politics all rolled into one.[5] The

3. Marantz.
4. Marantz.
5. Matthew Boyle, "Choke Artist: Hillary Clinton Has Yet Another Coughing Fit on Plane Ride from Ohio to Iowa," *Breitbart.com*, September 5,

picture of three coughing Hillarys accompanying the article worked to drive home these associations between illness, sex, and politics, as the images of Clinton holding her fist to her open mouth give an appearance of a gesture used to suggest giving a blow job. Such images were amplified on social media under the signs of #SickHillary and #HillarysHealth.

Clinton's "collapse" at the ceremonies commemorating the fifteenth anniversary of the attacks on September 11 in New York City ramped up the speculation further, as I will discuss below. Clinton and her campaign's explanation that she had pneumonia but tried to power through it was greeted with sympathy by some and suspicion by others. Trump was filmed at a rally in Pennsylvania making fun of Clinton's bout of pneumonia; he imitated her stumbling into her car to cheers from the crowd. Gifs of him imitating her collapse circulated on social media. Faced with criticism about his performance in the first debate on September 26, 2016, and images of him appearing to stalk Clinton aggressively on stage, Trump tried to turn the conversation about his own temperament and preparedness for the presidency into renewed speculation about "Hillary's health." And right-wing media and social media spread this speculation relentlessly.[6]

2016, https://www.breitbart.com/politics/2016/09/05/choke-artist-hillary -clinton-yet-another-coughing-fit-plane-ride-ohio-iowa/.

6. In one example of Trump's illness politics against Clinton, and its amplification in right-wing media, *The Gateway Pundit,* a notorious far-right news site, on October 15, 2016, published a brief article by the site's founder Jim Hoft with the title "Donald Trump Challenges #SickHillary to Drug Test before Debate!," https://www.thegatewaypundit.com/2016/10 /donald-trump-challenges-sickhillary-drug-test-debate/. After noting that, "Donald Trump spoke to a HUGE audience today in New Hampshire" (emphasis in original), Hoft writes, "The GOP nominee questioned why Hillary Clinton needs so many days off from campaigning each month?" Trump had tweeted that he and Clinton "should take a drug test" before the debates because he "didn't know what was going on" with Clinton. Calling for drug testing effectively sutures illness and criminalization.

Illness as Metaphor

While there was extensive coverage of the personal health of the presidential candidates in 2016 (and in 2020, as I will discuss in the next chapter), I was surprised by how little discussion there was in the media about the use of illness as metaphor in political rhetoric. In *Illness as Metaphor,* her now classic 1978 essay on the cultural politics of illness, Susan Sontag analyzed the phenomenon of illness as metaphor for individual and social weakness. Sontag's short book chronicles a long history of the metaphorical uses of illness in literature, popular culture, and politics. Her motivation for writing *Illness as Metaphor* was not simply to explore a changing cultural and political landscape of illness. Instead, with her already by then legendary bravado, Sontag proposed to elucidate the uses of illness as metaphor with the goal of purifying the experience of illness of metaphorical thinking. For Sontag, this was the "most truthful way of regarding illness—and the healthiest way of being ill."[7] And yet, despite her call for the de-metaphorization of the experience of illness, in many respects the opposite has happened in the four decades since she published her polemic: illness is now more metaphorized than ever. I argue that illness politics operates through the many sticky metaphors of illness, a process which Sontag's work helped illuminate.

7. Susan Sontag, *Illness as Metaphor* (New York: Farrar, Straus and Giroux, 1978), 3. I have written extensively about Sontag's work on illness in my book *Treatments: Language, Politics, and the Culture of Illness* (Minneapolis: University of Minnesota Press, 2007). In the chapter "Politicizing Patienthood: Ideas, Experience, Affect," I read Sontag's *Illness as Metaphor* and *AIDS and Its Metaphors* (New York: Farrar, Straus and Giroux, 1989) along with Audre Lorde's *The Cancer Journals* (San Francisco: Aunt Lute, 1980) and Eve Kosofsky Sedgwick's essay "White Glasses," first presented in 1991 and later published in her book *Tendencies* (Durham, N.C.: Duke University Press, 1993) as articulations of the politicization of patienthood. For more on the implications and impact of Sontag's rejection of metaphor, see Ann Jurecic, *Illness as Narrative* (Pittsburgh: University of Pittsburgh Press, 2012).

We can see this metaphorization of illness at work even in relation to the reception of Sontag's text, which has tended to focus on her metaphorical opening image more than her de-metaphorizing analysis. Sontag's opening metaphor suggests that health and illness are a kind of dual citizenship requiring two passports: "Although we all prefer to use only the good passport," she writes, "sooner or later each of us is obliged, at least for a spell, to identify ourselves as citizens of that other place."[8] In this metaphor, illness is "that other place," an authoritarian country that restricts freedom of thought and movement—that is, it is an embodiment of the political condition of unfreedom. The endurance of Sontag's ur-illness metaphor, as well as the failure of her intellectual argument against metaphorization, suggests the importance of the cultural work of illness and metaphor—and, indeed, illness metaphors—in contemporary social and political life.

In the 2016 race, both candidates sought to show their opponent as unfit for the presidency. Since even before he was candidate and Republican party nominee, Trump relied on a eugenics logic that portrays his opponents as weak, sick, and neurotic. For Trump, illness is a useful metaphor to suggest America's decline and the need for a powerful leader to purge the nation of weakness.[9] Before his focus on Clinton, Trump frequently suggested President Obama was a weak man whose presidency threatened the strength of the nation itself. Trump's birther conspiracy theories didn't simply seek

8. Sontag, *Illness as Metaphor,* 3.

9. In her book *Strongmen,* historian Ruth Ben-Ghiat discusses the rise of authoritarian rulers in the twentieth and twenty-first centuries. She describes the performance of virility as an important tool of authoritarian rule. Ben-Ghiat looks at the explicit display of sexual virility by rulers like Benito Mussolini, Silvio Berlusconi, and Donald Trump. She notes that "virility enables corruption, projecting the idea that he is above laws that weaker individuals must follow. It also translates into state policies that target women and LGBTQ+ populations, who are as much the strongman's enemies as prosecutors and the press," *Strongmen: Mussolini to the Present* (New York: Norton, 2020), 8. I would just add that, in the practice of virility politics, we also see a targeting and pathologization of ill and disabled people.

to question whether Obama was born in the United States; they also worked to draw attention to his mixed race and mixed national heritage, conjuring the specter of degeneration.

A similarly indirect association was at work in attempts to suggest Clinton was unfit. Her wealth of experience seemed to preclude a bluntly sexist dismissal of her as unqualified, but not an everyday sexism that also served as a dog whistle to conspiracy theories pushed by the alt-right that she was suffering from a degenerative disease thus far kept hidden from most Americans. There are numerous examples of what was a concerted Republican effort to create questions about Clinton's health and fitness for office, a strategy that combines sexism and ableism. By analyzing the illness politics deployed in the presidential election campaign in 2016, my intention is not simply to debunk the #SickHillary narrative. Rather, I want to ask more general questions about what makes a person fit for the presidency—or any job for that matter. What experiences prepare a person to lead and what experiences are perceived to be disqualifying? And how do we counter the ableist notion that illness and disability are disqualifying?

Clinton's Concussion

In Clinton's case, it is instructive to look back to the coverage of a health event in the media before she announced her run in 2016. In December 2012, then–Secretary of State Clinton fainted at home and hit her head. Her doctors Lisa Bardack and Gigi El-Bayoumi released a statement on December 15, 2012, explaining that she had fainted because of "extreme dehydration" from a stomach flu she had caught while traveling in Europe. They evaluated her and determined she had suffered a concussion. They recommended that she "rest and avoid strenuous activity."[10] This meant she was unable

10. Andrew Quinn, "Clinton Sustains Concussion; Benghazi Testimony Postponed," *Reuters*, December 15, 2012, https://www.reuters.com /article/us-usa-clinton/clinton-sustains-concussion-benghazi-testimony -postponed-idUSBRE8BE09Q20121216.

to continue testifying in the Benghazi hearings in the U.S. House of Representatives. Some right-wing media accused her of faking illness to avoid testifying. A *New York Post* editorial, for example, said "Clinton's story beggars belief," and in offering a summary of her story added ellipses, apparently to emphasize how dubious the story was, like a subtle eye roll after each clause: "While traveling in Europe, she contracted a stomach virus . . . which made her dehydrated . . . which made her faint at home . . . which caused her to fall and hit her head . . . which gave her a nasty concussion."[11] Thus, we see illness politics operating in the coverage of Clinton's health condition. Her doctors seek to present an aura of transparency and calm to dispel speculation and rumors while right-wing media immediately casts aspersions on the story. While the "faking it" accusation might seem at odds with later stories that she is hiding a secret illness, the point is in the rampant circulation, not the consistency of these illness stories.

And indeed the concussion would not be the end of the story. While monitoring her concussion, doctors found a blood clot in Clinton's brain. Her doctors issued another statement on December 31, 2012. I quote it here in full:

> In the course of a routine follow-up MRI on Sunday, the scan revealed that a right transverse sinus venous thrombosis had formed. This is a clot in the vein that is situated in the space between the brain and the skull behind the right ear. It did not result in a stroke, or neurological damage. To help dissolve this clot, her medical team began treating the Secretary with blood thinners. She will be released once the medication dose has been established. In all other aspects of her recovery, the Secretary is making excellent progress and we are confident she will make a full recovery. She is in good spirits, engaging with her doctors, her family, and her staff.[12]

11. "Hillary Clinton's Head Fake," *New York Post*, December 18, 2012, https://nypost.com/2012/12/18/hillary-clintons-head-fake/.

12. State Department Statement, December 31, 2012, https://2009-2017.state.gov/r/pa/prs/ps/2012/12/202419.htm.

In this statement, we see Clinton's doctors again offering clear information about her condition, treatment, and prognosis. With this further development and longer-term recovery, the initial story in the right-wing press that she was faking illness shifts to an accusation that she is hiding a more serious condition. Not surprisingly perhaps, social media became a space for speculation, and we see over the next several years a periodic resurgence of interest in Clinton's health and recurring references back to this incident as a means of discrediting her.

In 2014, for example, Republican strategist Karl Rove floated the possibility that Clinton had suffered "brain damage" in the fall. While, technically speaking, a concussion does of course do some, at least temporary, damage to the brain, Rove clearly used the term "brain damage" to seed doubt about Clinton's cognitive capacities. The *New York Post* quoted Rove voicing concerns about Clinton's condition at a conference: "Thirty days in the hospital? And when she reappears, she's wearing glasses that are only for people who have traumatic brain injury? We need to know what's up with that."[13] Rove would later walk back his remarks, admitting that Clinton was not in fact in the hospital for thirty days (it was only four), shifting to a vaguer, but still concerning, assertion that she spent a "30-day period fighting something."[14] Despite Rove walking back his comments, or indeed because of *how* he walked them back, which did little to dampen speculation, media coverage and social media commentary about her health continued.

Her glasses garnered much attention. An ABC News report in May 2014, for example, provides a timeline of her illness and even details when and where she wore "those now-famous glasses," as

13. Emily Smith, "Karl Rove: Hillary May Have Brain Damage," *New York Post*, May 12, 2014, https://pagesix.com/2014/05/12/karl-rove-hillary-clinton-may-have-brain-damage/.

14. Jon Greenberg, "Rove: Clinton Hospital Stay and Glasses Point to Traumatic Brain Injury," *PolitiFact* Truth-O-Meter, May 14, 2014, https://www.politifact.com/factchecks/2014/may/14/karl-rove/rove-clinton-hospital-stay-and-glasses-point-traum/.

the article describes them.[15] The timeline shows that Clinton returned to work on January 7, 2013, appeared in a photo-op without the glasses on January 9, and testified in the Benghazi hearing wearing the glasses, which, the timeline explains, led to "questions about her glasses." In response to these questions, State Department spokesperson Philippe Reines stated, "She'll be wearing these glasses instead of her contacts for a period of time because of lingering issues stemming from her concussion. With them on she sees just fine."[16] Clearly trying to use humor to dispel some of the hysteria surrounding the glasses, spokesperson Victoria Nuland repeated that "She sees just fine with them," and added, "she also enjoyed some of the comments she saw in the press about the extra sort of diplomatic lift she gets gesturing with them."[17] Humor would be a tactic Clinton and her team would use on several occasions to counteract rumors about her health, especially as a means to deflect Trump's frequent ableist jokes directed at her and what he persistently contended was her lack of stamina.[18]

Although Clinton would not officially announce her presidential bid until April 2015, even long before that announcement, most pundits thought she would run again in 2016, and thus we can see that an early and persistent Republican tactic to discredit her and her candidacy was to say she was both sick and hiding this fact. The notion that her glasses were a sign of both brain damage and deception about the damage, rather than a not very controversial means of alleviating some symptoms of concussion, shows how illness politics works via stigma and ableism. In his classic text on stigma, sociolo-

15. Mary Bruce, "Hillary Clinton Took 6 Months to 'Get Over' Concussion," *ABC News*, May 14, 2014, https://abcnews.go.com/blogs /politics/2014/05/hillary-clinton-took-6-months-to-get-over-concussion -bill-says-of-timeline.

16. Bruce.

17. Bruce.

18. For example, at the Al Smith Dinner in October 2016, Clinton said that Trump has been very concerned about her health and sent a car for her. The punchline: "It was a hearse." See Clinton deliver this joke here: https:// youtu.be/PUqOrnfpX2Q.

gist Erving Goffman describes stigma as "an undesired differentness from what is expected."[19] In his analysis, Goffman distinguished between two kinds of stigma—discredited and discreditable. Whereas discredited stigmas are visible, discreditable stigmas are those that are not immediately known or perceived but have the potential of being found out. In the alt-right-generated conspiracies regarding Clinton's health, her glasses, ironically, were theorized as a sign that allowed the public to see more clearly something that Clinton tried to keep hidden: that she was sick.

Stigma Power

Once Clinton was officially the Democratic nominee for President, Republican attacks on her fitness for office ramped up. It would be impossible to cover the multiplicity of allegations, but the general strategy of attack as we have already seen was consistent and had long been cultivated by Republican strategists like Rove: she had a problem in her brain, and she wasn't truthful about it. Following Imogen Tyler's important recent theorization of stigma as a key aspect of power, we might describe this as a form of "stigmacraft," or what Tyler describes as the use of stigma as a "technology of division and dehumanisation."[20] Tyler argues that "stigma power" is "crafted and cultivated as a means of leveraging political capital" and that the "exercise of stigma power is an integral component of [a recent] punitive authoritarian shift."[21] The circulation of misinformation and conspiracy theories is an exercise of stigma power. In

19. Erving Goffman, *Stigma Notes on the Management of Spoiled Identity* (New York: Simon and Schuster, 1963), 3.

20. Imogen Tyler, *Stigma: The Machinery of Inequality* (London: Zed, 2020). In her analysis, Tyler critiques Goffman for "unplug[ging] the concept of stigma from power: both the power-inflected microaggressions of the everyday social interactions that he was ostensibly interested in, and the larger structural and structuring power relations which shape the societies in which we live," 22.

21. Tyler, 7 and 19.

the case of Clinton's secret illness or illnesses, conspiracy theorists looked for (and found!) signs of illness and postulated at length on her methods of hiding illness. Like Kremlinologists trying to ascertain the health of aging Soviet leaders, people pored over still images and short videos for evidence of Clinton's secret illness. To understand how such speculation was fostered by the media and on social media, I will first look at coverage in August 2016 of photographs of Clinton purportedly needing help walking up a flight of stairs, before turning to some of the responses following Clinton's collapse at the ceremonies commemorating the fifteenth anniversary of September 11, 2001.

The photographs in question show Clinton climbing a short flight of stairs up to the front porch of a house in Charleston, South Carolina (Figure 1). One of the photos, by Reuters photographer Jonathan Ernst, shows Clinton, on the last step, slipping and reaching both arms out to staffers on either side of her to catch herself.

Figure 1. Photograph of Hillary Clinton slipping on steps while campaigning in Charleston, South Carolina in February 2016. REUTERS/Jonathan Ernst, https://www.snopes.com/fact-check/hillary-clinton-slipping-on-stairs/. Reprinted with permission of REUTERS/Jonathan Ernst.

Two male staffers offer support and help her keep her balance. Another man in front of her looks back and may also be reaching to help. Three men on the stairs to Clinton's right and a woman (Huma Abedin) behind on her left do not react to the stumble. The photograph was taken in February 2016 but resurfaced on social media that August, the timing of which indicates how the circulation and recirculation of images with very little context on social media is an effective way to encourage speculation and conspiracy theories.

On August 7, 2016, *The American Mirror*, a right-wing news source aggregator and blog created by Kyle Olsen, published a blog post with this photo and another taken just after of Clinton at the top of the stairs still holding on to the staffers on either side of her. Olsen's post argued that "the questionable health condition of Hillary Clinton should be a major issue in the 2016 campaign" and described the "latest evidence" as "Clinton being helped up a set of stairs by multiple individuals outside what appears to be a home."[22] Olsen's blog and tweets with the photo were then picked up and amplified by the conservative news source Drudge Report. The circulation of these images led to widespread discussion of Clinton's health on social media. This in turn led to other more mainstream media responding to the speculation generated by the right-wing blog and the Drudge Report. Brian Stelter, for example, covered the story for CNN in an article titled "Drudge Report Misleads Readers with Hillary Clinton Photo," which opens with this sentence: "From the looks of Matt Drudge's home page, Hillary Clinton is so sick, she needs help getting up a flight of stairs."[23] In his piece, Stelter

22. As reported with screen grabs from *The American Mirror* in Dan Evon, "Photograph of Hillary Clinton Slipping on Stairs Circulated as Proof of Poor Health," *Snopes.com*, August 8, 2016, https://www.snopes.com/fact -check/hillary-clinton-slipping-on-stairs/.

23. Brian Stelter, "Drudge Report Misleads Readers with Hillary Clinton Photo," *CNN*, August 8, 2016, https://money.cnn.com/2016/08/08 /media/drudge-report-hillary-clinton-fall/index.html. See also cover- age by the BBC and *Washington Post:* Tim Swift, "Clinton Health Myth," *BBC News*, August 19, 2016, https://www.bbc.com/news/election-us-2016

critiques the Drudge Report for intentionally misleading readers. But by presenting at face value the notion that the photo shows something remarkable rather than the hardly unusual situation of someone slipping on stairs and others responding to try to prevent a fall, such fact-checking pieces contribute to the wider circulation of unreliable sources, even as they discredit them.[24] Yet, I contend that we should also question more generally what is deemed disqualifying. Even if Clinton's slip were the result of, say, foot drop caused by a neurological condition, why would that be considered disqualifying of her ability to be president?[25] Weakness and vulnerability are stigmatized in American political culture, and this makes it difficult for a candidate for political office to be open about illness and disability. In this scenario, stigmatizing attitudes, rather than the illness or disability itself, become what disqualifies a person. This is what Tyler calls stigma power. And illness politics is a key component of the machinery of stigma power.

-37090082, and Ariana Eunjun Cha, "Don't Believe Everything You Read about Hillary Clinton's Health on Google," *Washington Post*, August 23, 2016, https://www.washingtonpost.com/news/to-your-health/wp/2016/08/22/dont-believe-everything-you-read-about-hillary-clintons-health-on-google/.

24. In her essay "*Gaslight* and the Shock Politics Two-Step," political theorist Bonnie Honig discusses how "truth requires an infrastructure, and popular subscription to it is one of truth's essential features," *Shell-Shocked: Feminist Criticism after Trump* (New York: Fordham University Press, 2021), 24. Thus, she argues, "holding the truth now means rebutting false claims of disinformation, but such rebuttals also energize false claims, increasing the life of their news cycle, widening their impact, and contributing further to a sense of helplessness and civic exhaustion," 25. We see this dynamic operating in relation to the illness politics used to discredit Clinton.

25. Full disclosure: I sometimes experience foot drop, because of a slipped disc in my cervical spine that protruded into and bruised my spinal cord. Surgery removed the disc and fused my cervical spine, but I still have some residual neurological symptoms, including weakness on my right side and occasional foot drop, both of which are more likely to appear if I'm tired or cold. I mention this not to diagnose Clinton as having disc issues in her cervical spine but simply to acknowledge how symptoms can be residual and intermittent and more or less apparent to others at different times.

Discussion of Clinton's health reached fever pitch after she collapsed at the ceremonies commemorating the fifteenth anniversary of September 11, 2001. WikiLeaks contributed to the speculation by tweeting an email from its cache of leaked Clinton emails and including the hashtag #HillarysHealth. The email dated January 4, 2013, was from Clinton's aide Huma Abedin to Clinton with the subject heading "Article I mentioned" and included the text of an article by Dr. Marc Siegel titled "Hillary Clinton's Blood Clot Treatment and the Need for Privacy," which was published by FOX News on January 3, 2013.[26] The WikiLeaks tweet did not provide any context for the article, simply noting that the article was about Clinton's "'life threatening' Sinus Thrombosis." Here we see WikiLeaks engaging in illness politics on social media by not only attempting to suggest that Clinton's collapse was related to her earlier sinus thrombosis, but also implying that Clinton's campaign was keeping important information about her health from the American public, and that this information was only now coming out thanks to the release of leaked emails by WikiLeaks beginning just before the Democratic National Convention in July.

Some replies to the WikiLeaks tweet point out that the article was from 2013 and not 2016 and questioned the timing of the tweet. If we actually read the article Abedin forwarded without comment to Clinton, we see that Siegel, who is identified as an associate professor of medicine and medical director of Doctor Radio at NYU Langone Medical Center, as well as "a member of the Fox News Medical A Team and author of *The Inner Pulse: Unlocking the Secret Code of Sickness and Health*," astutely and compassionately argues that Clinton's "illness is a reminder to all of us in the media, journalist and physician alike, that health care is primarily a private matter, not a time for lurid interest and certainly not a time

26. WikiLeaks, September 11, 2016, 5:50 pm, http://twitter.com /wikileaks.

for political criticism."[27] However, considering the timing of the WikiLeaks's tweet and the social and mainstream media attention the tweet generated, it is clear that WikiLeaks's intention was not to encourage understanding of illness as a private matter but instead to do the opposite: to generate "lurid interest" in the question of what is wrong with Clinton, as well as "political criticism" of her. And indeed, much commentary following the WikiLeaks tweet did indeed suggest that Abedin's email explained Clinton's collapse at the 9/11 commemoration in New York City, even if the article was three years old at the time.

To cite just one example of the coverage following the WikiLeaks tweet, an editorial by Kerry Jackson in *Investor's Business Daily* asked in its headline: "Is Hillary Clinton's Collapse Explained in Email from Huma Abedin?"[28] The headline itself makes it seem as though Abedin has herself written something in an email about Clinton's health rather than forwarding an article by a doctor about Clinton's fall, concussion, and blood clot published in January 2013. Jackson begins by acknowledging that "conspiracy theorists are having a grand ol' time trying to explain what was wrong with Hillary Clinton when she fainted/fell/collapsed/seized up during Sunday's 9/11 ceremony in New York."[29] He lists some of the theories about the incident and more general speculation about Clinton's health, which he says have raised questions about whether "she's suffering from dementia or Parkinson's disease—or

27. Huma Abedin email to Hillary Clinton, January 4, 2013, 5:10 pm. Copied into the text of the email is the article by Dr. Marc Siegel, "Hillary Clinton's Blood Clot Treatment and the Need for Privacy," *Fox News*, January 3, 2013, https://www.foxnews.com/health/hillary-clintons-blood -clot-treatment-and-the-need-for-privacy. Interestingly, when I searched online for this article, I discovered that the *Fox News* website now says this article was published on October 27, 2015.

28. Kerry Jackson, "Is Hillary Clinton's Collapse Explained in Email from Huma Abedin?" *Investor's Business Daily*, September 14, 2016, https://www.investors.com/politics/commentary/is-hillarys-collapse-explained-in -email-from-huma-abedin/.

29. Jackson.

possibly both."[30] Again, even as he seems to try to distance himself from the conspiracy theories, he shares them before arriving
at his main point: "But maybe the explanation is not so mysteri-
ous and is, in fact, hidden in plain sight."[31] The phrase "hidden in
plain sight" includes a hyperlink to the WikiLeaks tweet dated
September 11, 2016, of Abedin's email from 2013. Thus, Jackson's
editorial leads to the WikiLeaks tweet, which leads to the hashtag
#HillarysHealth. This is illness politics in action—two clicks and
readers enter an unfiltered world in which Hillary Clinton is diagnosed as sick and thus not fit to be president.

In his editorial, Jackson clearly states that the email from
2013 contains an article by Dr. Marc Siegel discussing "Clinton's
condition—right transverse sinus thrombosis." He then quotes
Siegel's description of sinus thrombosis and cites symptoms associated with the condition from Johns Hopkins Medicine's online
health resource. He also quotes Siegel in 2013 stating optimistical-
ly that Clinton "can look forward to a full recovery with the help
of her careful devoted physicians," and adds "so maybe Sunday's
episode wasn't related to what he discussed in his article." This
is followed by a big "but," wielded ominously: "But he also mentioned that she has a history of blood clots. Was her spell evidence
of another? The clots can return. Once treated doesn't always
mean healed."[32] "Once treated doesn't always mean healed" is
a not-so-subtle way to show how stigma operates as a sign that
sticks to and smears a person. Tyler says "stigma is a distinctly
psychosocial concept," and she adds that "it is important to pay
attention to stigma precisely because it captures the movement
between external and internal processes of de/valuation."[33] What
Jackson doesn't mention is Siegel's caution against just the sort of
speculative illness politics that the WikiLeaks tweet is aimed at

30. Jackson.
31. Jackson.
32. Jackson.
33. Tyler, *Stigma,* 239.

generating. That her aide would forward Clinton an article from a doctor discussing a condition she had been hospitalized for is hardly surprising or a sign of a secret being kept from the public. The irony is that Abedin's email, in which she forwards an article that ends with the sentence—"When it comes to celebrities and public leaders like Secretary Clinton, the urge to speculate and pontificate is high—but the high road is lined with respect and restraint"—would generate so much speculation and pontification three years after it was first published.

Later the same day that WikiLeaks tweeted Abedin's email with the article from Siegel (September 11, 2016), in a more explicit confirmation of its goal of encouraging lurid interest and political criticism of Clinton, Wikileaks tweeted a poll asking followers to respond to this prompt: "Hillary Clinton's collapse on Saturday, prior coughing fits & unusual facial & body movements are best explained by: Allergies & personality, Parkinsons, MS, Head injury complications."[34] Many tweets in response criticized the poll as inappropriate, especially for an organization purportedly interested in transparency. Brandy Jensen (@BrandyLJensen) replied with a tweet that went viral and pointed to the sexual politics that also seemed at play in WikiLeaks's targeting of Clinton: "WikiLeaks is the internet's deeply embarrassing ex-boyfriend." WikiLeaks would eventually delete the tweet with the poll, admitting that the poll was too "speculative."[35] Yet, even in retracting their Twitter poll as too speculative, WikiLeaks effectively encouraged speculation and mistrust of what by then was the explanation given by the Clinton team: that Clinton had been suffering from pneumonia and had tried to work through it. WikiLeaks's poll worked like Rove's earlier brain damage comment: it suggested something was wrong

34. WikiLeaks, September 11, 2016, 11:37 pm, http://twitter.com/wikileaks.

35. For coverage of the tweet, see Marcus Gilmer, "Wikileaks Retracts Twitter Poll Speculating about Clinton's Health," *Mashable*, September 11, 2016, https://mashable.com/article/wikileaks-hillary-clinton-health-poll.

with Clinton, belittled her for her condition (whatever it might be), and encouraged rumors to circulate even though the tweet was eventually deleted.

Diagnosing by GIF

In alt-right media, Clinton was constantly being "diagnosed by gif," a phrase I use to describe the visual cultural phenomenon of using a brief clip of video shown on loop as evidence indicating a symptom of a health condition. In delineating the workings of stigma, Tyler writes that her book "seeks to capture some of the cultural practices that characterize the intensification of stigma politics in the current conjuncture, including the ascendance of stigmatising media and cultural genres: 'stigmatainments' in which the public are called upon to perform roles as angry and outraged citizens."[36] I would argue that diagnosing by gif is a form of stigmatainment, and we saw it in action in relation to Clinton in numerous ways. For example, there are many gifs purporting to be incontrovertible evidence of Clinton having a seizure on camera. My personal favorite is the use of a video loop of Clinton at the Democratic National Convention reacting to the balloon drop as evidence of her alleged seizure disorder. In this and other examples, Clinton's most human gestures are pathologized—in this case, a goofy reaction to the huge number of balloons dropping from the ceiling was deemed symptomatic of illness in a way that, say, Tim Kaine's similarly goofy responses were not.

In some cases, everyday sexism served to mask an illness-conspiracy dog whistle, as when Reince Priebus commented on Clinton not smiling during the Commander-in-Chief forum.[37] On the one hand, this was clearly meant to provoke an angry response to the sexist demand from men that women smile. On the other, it

36. Tyler, *Stigma*, 26.
37. Reince Priebus, September 7, 2016, 9:27pm, http://twitter.com /reince.

gestured to fervent alt-right social media discussion about Clinton's lack of facial expressivity that was explained as a symptom of Parkinson's disease. One might note that Clinton's goofy reaction to the balloons dropping contradicts the allegation that she lacks facial expressivity, but again, contradictory messages generate rather than squelch speculation. Moreover, women politicians have long had to try to walk a very fine line in terms of what is considered suitable emotional expression as they seek public office. A woman candidate is damned if does emotion and damned if she doesn't. My point is that in these associations, sexual politics becomes illness politics. In 2016, these hidden illness narratives worked to further the impression Trump's campaign wanted to give that Clinton was unfit because she couldn't handle the physical demands of the office—she lacked stamina in Trump's oft-repeated accusation—and she was keeping secrets from us. Here again we see illness politics in action, with illness crafted as an outward sign of not only physical but also moral weakness. In the next chapter, I show how Trump, who had been an astute practitioner of illness politics in 2016, became a target of its stigma power in 2020 through the hashtag #TrumpIsNotWell.

2. #TrumpIsNotWell

IN BOTH THE 2016 AND 2020 CAMPAIGNS, Trump, too, was diagnosed as unfit for office. If the weak Obama and sick Hillary illness narratives conjured an older eugenics logic that Trump himself adhered to and promulgated, initial attacks on Trump's fitness in the run-up to the 2016 election and after drew on a newer narrative—that of the personality disorder. Disability activists and scholars rightly expressed concern that diagnosing Trump's bad behavior as mental illness was stigmatizing to people who suffer from mental illness. And yet, in a fascinating reversal of stigmatization, or perhaps as a sign of Trump's own savvy use of stigma power, the diagnosis of Trump's purported narcissistic personality disorder was not without its benefits for the candidate himself. In pop psychology and culture, such powerful if unpleasant personalities have been linked to success, especially in the business world. In an interview on *Good Morning America* in September 2016, Trump described his temperament in business terms as "the single greatest asset I have," using a tried-and-true interview tactic of turning a potential weakness into a purported strength—no doubt such a response was second nature for Trump, drawing on his long experience in business and as star of the reality TV show *The Apprentice*.[1] In this instance, he

1. Rebecca Savransky, "Trump: My Temperament 'Single Greatest Asset,'" *The Hill*, September 6, 2016, https://thehill.com/blogs/ballot-box /presidential-races/294556-trump-my-temperament-single-greatest-asset/.

sought to counter Clinton's questioning of his temperament, which included the now oft-repeated one-liner: "A man you can bait with a tweet should not be trusted with nuclear weapons."[2] In the same interview, Trump dismissed Clinton as "not having a presidential look," which we might see as yet another example of his wielding of stigma power "as a means of leveraging political capital"[3] through a combination of sexism and ableism. What does a president look like, after all? Trump offers yet another version of a not-so-subtle eugenics logic in the form of a white, male identity politics: the unsaid of Trump's dig of course is that a president looks like him, not like Clinton or Obama.

Trump's Mockery of Disability

During the 2016 campaign and continuing into his presidency, questions about Trump's mental health were a media mainstay. Again, disability scholars and activists argued that the problem is not that Trump is mentally ill but that he is a bigot with authoritarian tendencies and that, in opposing him, activists should focus on his ableist policies not his personality. Despite this push by disabled activists to focus on his policies, Trump mocking a disabled reporter in November 2015 on the campaign trail in South Carolina became one of the lasting images from the 2016 presidential campaign.[4] Although I agree with disabled activists on this point, I do

2. Savransky. With Trump's ongoing attempts to overturn the 2020 election, Clinton's zinger is still frequently cited on social media.

3. Tyler, *Stigma*, 7.

4. "Donald Trump Accused of Mocking Reporter with a Disability," *ABC News*, November 27, 2015, https://www.youtube.com/watch?v=hFOy8 -03qdg. The *ABC News* clip on YouTube notes in the description that, "The Republican presidential candidate has insisted he never met the New York Times reporter, Serge F. Kovaleski." According to Kovaleski, the two "were on a first-name basis for years." He added, "I've interviewed him in his office. I've talked to him at press conferences. All in all, I would say around a dozen times, I've interacted with him as a reporter while I was at *The Daily News*," Maggie Haberman, "Donald Trump Says His Mocking of New York

want to look back briefly at the incident as an example of illness politics and because people tend not to remember the context of Trump's mockery of *New York Times* reporter Serge Kovaleski, who has arthrogryposis, a condition that involves joint contracture and stiffness. At the rally in South Carolina, Trump was repeating his anti-Muslim assertion that "thousands and thousands of people were cheering" in Jersey City, New Jersey, when the World Trade Center was attacked and collapsed on September 11, 2001. Trump claimed to have seen these celebrations on television and cited as additional evidence a story written by Kovaleski and Fredrick Kunkle in the *Washington Post* that mentioned an FBI investigation into a possible terrorist cell operating in northern New Jersey. In that article, Kovaleski and Kunkle wrote, "In Jersey City, within hours of two jetliners' plowing into the World Trade Center, law enforcement authorities detained and questioned a number of people who were allegedly seen celebrating the attacks and holding tailgate-style parties on rooftops while they watched the devastation on the other side of the river."[5] When asked about the article later, Kovaleski said he couldn't recall the exact details of his reporting but denied that there was evidence of widespread celebrations. As is clear from the article itself, "a number of people" is not "thousands and thousands," but that hasn't stopped Trump from continuing to maintain that he saw thousands and thousands of Muslims celebrating on September 11, 2001. I bring this story up not to rehash one of Trump's favorite false claims. As Bonnie Honig has shown convincingly, through his constant tweeting, as well as through his rallies and the clips that would circulate after, Trump

Times Reporter Was Misread," *New York Times,* November 26, 2015, https:// www.nytimes.com/2015/11/27/us/politics/donald-trump-says-his-mocking -of-new-york-times-reporter-was-misread.html.

5. Serge Kovaleski and Fredrick Kunkle, "Northern New Jersey Draws Probers' Eyes," *The Washington Post*, September 18, 2001, https://www .washingtonpost.com/archive/politics/2001/09/18/northern-new-jersey -draws-probers-eyes/40f82ea4-e015-4d6e-a87e-93aa433fafdc/?itid=lk _inline_manual_39.

has practiced adeptly as both candidate and president what Honig calls the "shock politics two-step," which combines disorientation and desensitization in a mechanism that exhausts people into submission. I want to connect my concept and practice of illness politics with Honig's shock politics two-step by noting how, in Trump's performance at the rally in South Carolina in 2015, ableism is used to discredit a reporter's trustworthiness and as validation of Trump's racism. Here we see stigma power in action: Trump's performance of bigotry and bullying is expressed through a (verbal and visual) suturing of racism and ableism.

Polls showed most Americans did not like that Trump made fun of a person's disability. In a Bloomberg Politics poll in August 2016, for example, a higher percentage of Americans said "Trump's criticism of a reporter that was seen as mocking the reporter's physical disability" bothered them more than any other incident or position mentioned by pollsters.[6] Only 15 percent said the mockery did not bother them at all. Yet, even despite the polling showing widespread disapproval of Trump's mocking of disability, Trump would demonstrate a similar show of contempt for apparent weakness when he imitated Clinton's collapse at the fifteenth anniversary of September 11, as I discussed in the last chapter. It is possible that at least some Americans were less concerned about Trump's personal attacks on the fitness of his opponent (politics can be dirty, after all) but found his belittling imitation of Kovaleski to be reprehensible. Still, it's important to note that disability activists consistently tried to turn the conversation from the spectacle of Trump's mockery of disability to the ableism of Trump's policies, including, for example, the proposed replacement plan for the Affordable Care Act (ACA). I will explore some of the activism to save the ACA led by disabled people in the next chapter when I turn my analysis away from electoral politics and toward illness and disability activism.

6. John McCormick, "Clinton Up 6 on Trump in Two-way Race in Bloomberg National Poll," *Bloomberg*, August 10, 2016, https://www.bloomberg.com/news/articles/2016-08-10/bloomberg-politics-national-poll.

Mental Health Professionals and the Goldwater Rule

Speculation about Trump's fitness for office continued after he was elected president in 2016. Shortly after his inauguration, a group of thirty-five psychiatrists, psychologists, and social workers published a letter in the *New York Times* challenging the American Psychiatric Association's Goldwater Rule, which they described as a "self-imposed dictum about evaluating public figures."[7] In the brief letter, the mental health professionals offered the following diagnosis of Trump:

> Mr. Trump's speech and actions demonstrate an inability to tolerate views different from his own, leading to rage reactions. His words and behavior suggest a profound inability to empathize. Individuals with these traits distort reality to suit their psychological state, attacking facts and those who convey them (journalists, scientists).
>
> In a powerful leader, these attacks are likely to increase, as his personal myth of greatness appears to be confirmed. We believe that the grave emotional instability indicated by Mr. Trump's speech and actions makes him incapable of serving safely as president.[8]

Tellingly, there is no mention of Trump's policies in the letter, only a vague reference twice to "Mr. Trump's speech and actions." Psychological language is used instead, presumably to give authority to the diagnosis: "rage reactions," "profound inability to empathize," "distort reality," "personal myth of greatness," and "grave emotional instability." Here, the psychological becomes political. In proposing the revocation of the Goldwater Rule, the letter writers argue that they have a public duty to diagnose someone who, based on their psychological training, they are convinced is a danger to society.

In another letter to the editor of the *New York Times* in response to this group letter from his professional colleagues, Dr. Allen

7. Lance Dodes and Joseph Schachter, "Mental Health Professionals Warn about Trump," *New York Times*, February 13, 2017, https://www.nytimes.com/2017/02/13/opinion/mental-health-professionals-warn-about-trump.html.

8. Dodes and Schachter.

Frances, emeritus professor of psychiatry and behavioral sciences at Duke University and chairperson of the task force that wrote the *Diagnostic and Statistical Manual of Mental Disorders IV,* responded to the "fevered media speculation about Donald Trump's psychological motivations and psychiatric diagnosis" that had led some mental health professionals to weigh in publicly on questions about Trump's mental health.[9] Dr. Frances argued that Trump should be taken to task not for being "crazy" but for behaving badly. His letter was prompted by concern for the fact that mental health professionals were disregarding "the usual ethical constraints against diagnosing public figures at a distance."[10] This concern, however, did not stop Dr. Frances from asserting in no uncertain terms that Trump does not have narcissistic personality disorder, because, well, as he asserted, I should know, I'm the person who wrote the criteria on NPD. Dr. Frances ends his letter by arguing that the "antidote to a dystopic Trumpean dark age is political, not psychological."[11] While I don't disagree with Frances's call to do politics, I would also contend that it is not possible to separate the psychological from the political. I say: do politics, yes, but this includes illness politics, and by this I mean, consider how illness is used politically in tandem with race, gender, sexuality, and class.

In drawing attention to the illness politics surrounding both Clinton, discussed in the last chapter, and Trump in this chapter, it is helpful to consider the uses of illness as metaphor in 2016 within the context of a longer history of illness politics. The references to the American Psychiatric Association's Goldwater Rule in relation to Trump suggest some of this longer history. In a press release in March 2017, the APA reaffirmed support for the Goldwater Rule,

9. Allen Frances, "An Eminent Psychiatrist Demurs on Trump's Mental State," *New York Times,* February 14, 2017, https://www.nytimes.com/2017/02/14/opinion/an-eminent-psychiatrist-demurs-on-trumps-mental-state.html.

10. Frances.

11. Frances.

writing, "The American Psychiatric Association (APA) today reaffirmed its support behind the ethics guideline commonly known as 'The Goldwater Rule,' which asserts that member psychiatrists should not give professional opinions about the mental state of someone they have not personally evaluated."[12] The APA's news release provides a brief history of the Goldwater Rule, explaining that in the 1964 presidential election, *Fact* magazine had polled over 12,000 psychiatrists about whether presidential candidate Senator Barry Goldwater was "psychologically fit to be president. A total of 2,417 of those queried responded, with 1,189 saying that Goldwater was unfit to assume the presidency. Goldwater would later sue the magazine, which was found liable for damages."[13] The Goldwater Rule was first implemented by the APA in 1973. In reaffirming the Goldwater Rule, the APA clarified and even expanded the rationale for the decision as follows:

1. When a psychiatrist comments about the behavior, symptoms, diagnosis, etc. of a public figure without consent, that psychiatrist has violated the principle that psychiatric evaluations be conducted with consent or authorization.
2. Offering a professional opinion on an individual that a psychiatrist has not examined is a departure from established methods of examination, which require careful study of medical history and first-hand examination of the patient. Such behavior compromises both the integrity of the psychiatrist and the profession.
3. When psychiatrists offer medical opinions about an individual they have not examined, they have the potential to stigmatize those with mental illness.[14]

Debate and discussion over the APA's stance would continue throughout Trump's presidency, culminating in a fierce denunci-

12. "APA Reaffirms Support for Goldwater Rule," March 16, 2017, https://psychiatry.org/news-room/news-releases/apa-reaffirms-support -for-goldwater-rule.

13. "APA Reaffirms Support for Goldwater Rule."

14. "APA Remains Committed to Supporting Goldwater Rule," March 16, 2017, https://psychiatry.org/news-room/apa-blogs/apa-blog/2017/03 /apa-remains-committed-to-supporting-goldwater-rule.

ation of the APA's reaffirmation and clarification of the Goldwater Rule by Trump's niece Mary L. Trump, who has a PhD in Psychology. In an op-ed in the *Washington Post* in October 2020, Mary Trump argued that the APA's stance not only prohibited members from diagnosing public figures, but it also now meant "they could no longer offer a professional opinion of any sort, no matter how well supported or evidence-based, even if they believed that a public figure posed a threat to the country's citizens or national security."[15] Here again we see illness politics in action in relation to the contested political uses and abuses of diagnosis.

Illness politics was also at work in the 1960 presidential election. In one of his "Doctor's World" columns in the *New York Times* published a month before the 1992 presidential election, Lawrence K. Altman, M.D., discussed what the article's title identified as the "disturbing issue of Kennedy's secret illness." Altman noted that "many Presidents have suffered serious illness while in the White House. All too often they, their families and aides have misled, if not lied to, the public about their health, with the malady becoming known only many years later."[16] Altman goes on to discuss a then just-published report in the *Journal of the American Medical Association* in which pathologists who were at John F. Kennedy's autopsy revealed that Kennedy's adrenal glands were "almost completely gone," confirming that he had Addison's disease, a diagnosis he and his family had always denied, including during the 1960 presidential election.[17] As Altman explains, if the public had known

15. Mary L. Trump, "Psychiatrists Know What's Wrong with My Uncle. Let Them Tell Voters," *The Washington Post*, October 22, 2020, https://www .washingtonpost.com/outlook/psychiatrists-mary-trump-goldwater/2020/10 /22/ebf5e2b6-13c0-11eb-ba42-ec6a580836ed_story.html.

16. Lawrence K. Altman, "The Doctor's World; Disturbing Issue of Kennedy's Secret Illness," *The New York Times*, October 6, 1992, https:// www.nytimes.com/1992/10/06/health/the-doctor-s-world-disturbing-issue -of-kennedy-s-secret-illness.html.

17. Dennis L. Breo, "JFK's Death: The Plain Truth from the MDs Who Did the Autopsy," *JAMA: The Journal of the American Medical Association* 267, no. 20 (May 27, 1992), 2794.

in 1960 that Kennedy had Addison's, he might have lost what was a very close election to Richard Nixon.

Altman points out that since 1960 there has been an "enormous expansion of coverage of health issues" in the media,[18] and I contend that the 1960s and 1970s is also the moment when illness (both mental and physical) begins to figure as a site of political struggle, though it has been largely overshadowed in contemporary interpretations of the period by a focus on gender, race, and sexuality as sites of struggle. Many have noted that Trump's call to "make America great again" is an attempt to hearken back to a 1950s America that is more fantasy than reality. The illness politics of the 2016 presidential election suggest a wish by some to go back in time to before 1960, to before the rise of the new social movements that made it possible for us to have the first African American president and (almost) the first woman president. Recall

18. Altman, "Doctor's World." I am arguing that coverage of health issues has expanded even further since Altman was writing in the early 1990s, what with the rise of the cable news industry in the 1990s and social media in the 2000s. Altman's column is an early example of a doctor commentariat, a phenomenon that also featured prominently in the 2016 election, as the example of Dr. Mehmet Oz's "examination" of Trump's health data. As I was writing this in 2022, Dr. Oz was the Republican candidate for the U.S. Senate in Pennsylvania. Oz engaged in his own illness politics against his opponent John Fetterman, who had a stroke in May 2022 just after he had won the Democratic party nomination. One of Oz's senior advisors, Rachel Tripp, in a response to humorous attacks from Fetterman's camp on a video of Oz at a grocery store expressing shock at the price of "crudités," said, "If John Fetterman had ever eaten a vegetable in his life, then maybe he wouldn't have had a major stroke and wouldn't be in the position of having to lie about it constantly," Madeline Berg, "Oz Campaign on Fetterman: If He'd 'Eaten a Vegetable,' He Wouldn't Have Had a Stroke," *Business Insider*, August 23, 2022, https://www.businessinsider.com/oz-on-fetterman-if-hed -eaten-vegetable-wouldnt-have-stroke-2022-8. Here illness politics stands in for a crude class politics that stigmatizes poverty. At the same time, we see the articulation of the ideological position that health is a matter of personal responsibility. This very clear example of illness politics was happening as I was finishing this book, so I was unable to showcase this story, but I do briefly return to Fetterman's campaign and victory over Oz in chapter 4.

Trump's comment that Clinton did not have a "presidential look" as a counterattack to her attempts to portray him as not having the right temperament to be president.

Weaponizing Weakness

If initial doubts about Trump's fitness for office tended to focus on his temperament and narcissistic personality, in 2020 we saw an increasing number of attempts to portray him as not only temperamentally but also physically unfit for office. These attacks resembled some of the illness politics used to generate uncertainty and concern about Clinton's health in 2016 under the hashtags #SickHillary and #HillarysHealth, as discussed in the last chapter. We saw a similar illness politics at work against Trump when clips from a commencement speech he gave at the United States Military Academy on June 13, 2020, circulated widely on social media. The clips seemed to indicate Trump had difficulty drinking water and walking down a ramp. Just days after Trump's speech at West Point, the Lincoln Project, a group whose stated mission was to "defeat President Trump and Trumpism at the ballot box," released a forty-five-second mash-up video designed to weaponize weakness as a form of illness politics.[19] The video was merciless: "He's shaky. He's weak," the voiceover intoned, visually connecting physical decline with moral decay. The irony, of course, is that weaponizing weakness, or a perception of weakness, had been, and still is, one of Trump's signature political strategies. The clip of Trump drinking lasts approximately three seconds, while the clip of Trump walking down a ramp lasts fifteen seconds. In no time, then, word and images are out: Trump is not well. The evidence can be watched on loop and shared easily via hashtag. Repeat and retweet after me: #TrumpIsNotWell. Trump, like Clinton, was diagnosed by gif, and hoist on his own ableist petard.

19. Lincoln Project, "#TrumpIsNotWell," June 16, 2020, https://www.youtube.com/watch?v=NVy_LWM091g.

The Lincoln Project was organized by a group of Republicans disenchanted by the direction Trump had taken their party. In a feature about the Lincoln Project in *The New Yorker* in October 2020, Paige Williams describes the group as "a super PAC of Republican operatives who have disavowed their own party in order to defeat President Donald Trump."[20] She explains that the group's founders, including Republican consultants Steve Schmidt and Rick Wilson, decided to call themselves the Lincoln Project in order to invoke the Republican party's connection to Abraham Lincoln and "weaponize it."[21] She also describes their media and social media tactics as influenced by their study of "a combat technique, developed after the Korean War, called the *ooda* loop—Observe, Orient, Decide, and Act—in which a fighter outmaneuvers an opponent by processing and acting on information quickly, rather than waiting to develop a definitive assessment. Such a rapid offense is meant to disorient and overwhelm a target. The Project's strategists metabolize news quickly enough to create spots within hours, or even minutes, of an event."[22]

Here we have an example of what philosopher Michel Foucault described in his lectures at the Collège de France in 1976 as an inversion of Carl von Clausewitz's famous dictum: not "war is politics by other means" but "politics is the continuation of war by other means."[23] Of course, the strategy deployed by the Lincoln Project is not so unlike Trump's own use of Twitter as, in Bonnie Honig's analysis, "a *device of disorientation,* blocking access to the solitude and plurality that are the conditions of critical thinking and reflection."[24] Indeed, in a piece for *Sidecar,* the *New Left Review* blog,

20. Paige Williams, "Inside the Lincoln Project's War against Trump," *The New Yorker,* October 5, 2020, https://www.newyorker.com/magazine /2020/10/12/inside-the-lincoln-projects-war-against-trump.

21. Williams.

22. Williams.

23. Michel Foucault, *"Society Must Be Defended": Lectures at the Collège de France, 1975–76,* trans. David Macey (New York: Picador, 2003), 15.

24. Honig, *Shell-Shocked,* 17.

Michael Hardt, drawing on Foucault's lectures, asserts that, "One principle that gives relative coherence to the political rationality of the Trump faction is this: politics is merely the continuation of war by other means."[25] Thus, it makes sense to me that it would be Republican operatives who would seek to discredit Trump through a combative illness politics that weaponizes weakness, in this case, Trump's own weakness.

The example Williams gives of this combat technique in action on social media is the Lincoln Project's video and hashtag #TrumpIsNotWell. As Williams explains, "The viral spot subjected the President to one of his own tricks: he mocked Hillary Clinton when she stumbled in 2016, and constantly suggests that Biden is senile. Trump was soon wasting time at a campaign rally defending his ability to walk and to drink water."[26] Williams doesn't spend any more time analyzing the #TrumpIsNotWell video: both Trump and the Lincoln Project are presented as mocking their opponents by highlighting moments of weakness and vulnerability. The story Williams tells is one of comeuppance for a bully: Trump getting a taste of his own medicine from the Lincoln Project. In her discussion of the different types of videos the Lincoln Project has produced, and the multiple intended audiences for various videos, Williams explains that some are produced for an "audience of one"—that is, their goal is to "destabilize Trump" like a "military 'PsyOp.'"[27] While the #TrumpIsNotWell ad clearly had a broader audience in mind, it also worked through stigma and ableism as a means to humiliate Trump. In one three-second shot, for example, we see the legs of a man from behind as he climbs the steps up to an airplane—presumably Trump boarding Air Force One, but we never see his head, so we can't say for sure. The video gag is that

25. Michael Hardt, "War by Other Means," *Sidecar, New Left Review* blog, January 21, 2021, https://newleftreview.org/sidecar/posts/war-by -other-means.

26. Williams, "Inside the Lincoln Project's War against Trump."

27. Williams.

the footage has captured the president with a piece of white paper—haha toilet paper!—stuck to his shoe. The voiceover during this sequence says, "Why do so many reporters who cover the White House pretend they can't see Trump's decline?" As with Clinton slipping as she goes up a flight of stairs, the question to ask is: how and why is this a sign of decline?

As in 2016, many disabled writers and activists immediately objected to the Lincoln Project's #TrumpIsNotWell ad and the ableist attitudes that the tactic of weaponizing perceived physical weakness reveals. Disability advocates like Rebecca Cokely, director of the Disability Justice Initiative at the Center for American Progress, rightly argued that the focus on Trump's difficulty drinking water and walking down a ramp detracted from the real issues, including that his policies and positions have been harmful to disabled and chronically ill people.[28] Senator Tammy Duckworth (D-Illinois), who was disabled in combat and uses a wheelchair, also called out the ableism of the clips on Twitter, retweeting David A. Graham's article in *The Atlantic* which offers a more extended case as to why the "search for some disqualifying physical ailment is a distraction."[29]

Visual tactics like freezing and looping, cutting and splicing, slowing down and speeding up, all of which amount to forms of manipulation—or "doctoring"—of evidence are used to help us see something that we are led to believe might otherwise remain unseen. Put all together, we viewers participate in the practice I have been calling "diagnosing by gif," in which a short video played on loop allegedly reveals a person's secret illness and related moral failing. The Lincoln Project's #TrumpIsNotWell ad is a clas-

---

28. Rebecca Cokley, "Calling Trump Unwell Doesn't Hurt Trump. It Hurts Disabled People," *The Washington Post*, June 16, 2020, https://www.washingtonpost.com/outlook/2020/06/16/mock-trump-hurts-disabled/.

29. David A. Graham, "Trump's West Point Stumbles Aren't the Problem," *The Atlantic*, June 15, 2020, https://www.theatlantic.com/ideas/archive/2020/06/trump-ramp/613051/.

sic of the genre. "Trump doesn't have the strength to lead. Nor the character to admit it," the ad tells us, directly linking physical ability with moral character (Figure 2). The images accompanying these two statements are of Trump yet again appearing to have difficulty drinking followed by the by-now oft-repeated image of Trump mocking Serge Kovaleski. The ad creates a chain of verbal and visual associations connecting Trump's supposed physical weakness with his mocking of disability. The juxtaposition of images suggests that the best way to respond to Trump's mockery is with more mockery of his own weakness and disability. Social media is then used to circulate the ad quickly and widely and generate increasing doubt about Trump's health via the hashtag #TrumpIsNotWell.

The Lincoln Project understood this process well and frequently shared the forty-five-second video on Twitter. In one instance, for example, they shared the video and repeated speculation from the ad about a visit Trump had made to Walter Reed: "Why did Trump have a secretive, midnight run to Walter Reed Medical Center?," the tweet asked, adding, "It's time to talk about it. #TrumpIsNotWell."[30] In the video, when this question is asked, we see a short two-second clip repeated twice—the first repetition of the clip shows Trump at a distance walking toward a black SUV with what appear to be two Secret Service officers on duty, one along the path Trump walks and the other standing guard at the back of the SUV; the second zooms in to give us a closer look at Trump. There is clearly a bright sun in the footage, shining on Trump's face, casting shadows, and creating a reflection on the SUV, so we are not witnessing the midnight run itself, though perhaps this is the morning after the midnight run? When the video zooms in, what are we meant to see? Trump gazes downward, is hunched a bit forward as he walks, and he seems to frown, but there is no way for me to tell that this is showing a

Figure 2. Screen grab from the Lincoln Project's #TrumpIsNotWell video. At a speech at the United States Military Academy on June 13, 2020, Trump appears to have difficulty lifting a water bottle to his mouth to drink. In the Lincoln Project's ad, the voiceover tells the viewer, "Trump doesn't have the strength to lead." The Lincoln Project, June 16, 2020, https://twitter.com/ProjectLincoln/status /1273028594432958467.

person who is sick, without the voiceover and tweet urging me to make this association. As in my analysis of similar tactics of illness politics used against Clinton in 2016, I believe that it is crucial that we understand these visual tactics so that we do not fall prey to the spurious message that illness and disability make a person unfit for public office.

Diagnosing by video is not a new political tactic. I first became interested in this phenomenon in 2005 in relation to the use of a videotape provided to the media by the parents of Terri Schiavo as evidence that she was not brain dead. I have written at greater length about the Schiavo case as a "mediatized medical event,"[31] but here I

31. Lisa Diedrich, "Speeding Up Slow Deaths: Medical Sovereignty circa 2005," *MediaTropes* eJournal 2, no. 1 (2011): 1–22, https://mediatropes .com/index.php/Mediatropes/article/view/15744. In this earlier piece, I

simply want to mention some of the ways illness politics operated visually in this case. Although social media was only just emerging at the time, images from the videotape of Schiavo were shown over and over on cable television, often in a constant loop as background to reporting on the story. In another twist, Senator Bill Frist, a former transplant surgeon and at the time presidential candidate, took to the Senate floor to proclaim that Schiavo was not in a persistent vegetative state. His diagnosis was based on his examination of the videotape, not of Schiavo herself. Although he hoped his diagnosis of Schiavo would breathe life into his presidential campaign, Frist was widely criticized for this stunt. Moreover, although there was clearly sympathy for Schiavo's parents throughout the case, the images of Schiavo on loop did not generate recognition among the public so much as fear of her condition and horror at the media spectacle surrounding it, as the increase in calls to the National Hospice and Palliative Care Organization's (NHPCO) helpline before and after Schiavo's death indicated.[32]

The looping phenomenon has since become standard fare on 24–7 cable news channels. Now with social media, the phenomenon is more condensed and concentrated, and images can circulate even more widely. Looping and other visual techniques direct our attention to something that has been made visible that we too can now see. Look closely. Look again. There it is: Donald Trump mentally

---

juxtaposed analyses of the Terri Schiavo case and Hurricane Katrina and its aftermath, both of which took place in 2005, as "mediatized medical events," which I defined "as events in which the practices of medicine received considerable media attention at a particular historical moment; or, we might say, as events that brought a convergence between media and medical practices," 1.

32. Jane Erikson, "Terri Schiavo Impact Continues One Year after Her Death," *Oncology Times* 28, no. 5 (March 10, 2006): 6–7, https://journals.lww .com/oncology-times/fulltext/2006/03100/terri_schiavo_impact_continues _one_year_after_her.5.aspx.

and physically declining, Hillary Clinton having a seizure,[33] Nancy Pelosi slurring her words,[34] Biden suffering from dementia.[35]

"We're not doctors," the Lincoln Project video admits, as it shows an image of Trump's doctor Harold Bornstein.[36] This visual gag plays on the assumption that we can see for ourselves that Bornstein doesn't look much like a "typical" doctor, visually calling into question his diagnosis of Trump as fit. "But, we're not blind." In other words, we are not disabled and thus, we—and now you too—can diagnose Trump. It helps to recall that the verb "to doctor" means both "to restore to good condition" and "to adapt or modify for a desired end." Diagnosing by gif is a form of doctoring—"to alter deceptively"—because it takes a brief moment out of context that focuses the viewer's attention on a sign that is then claimed to be symptomatic of a personal problem. This is what we need to see better: Using visual tactics promotes an illness politics that weaponizes weakness and limits our image of what makes a leader. Only when we recognize this, can we begin to counteract the ableism that undergirds and undermines our politics.

33. Lisa Lerer, "No, Hillary Clinton Is Not Having a Seizure in That Video, Says AP Reporter Who Was There," *Chicago Tribune,* August 13, 2016, https://www.chicagotribune.com/opinion/commentary/ct-hillary-clinton -health-20160812-story.html.

34. Drew Harwell, "Faked Pelosi Videos, Slowed to Make Her Appear Drunk, Spread across Social Media," *The Washington Post,* May 24, 2019, https://www.washingtonpost.com/technology/2019/05/23/faked-pelosi -videos-slowed-make-her-appear-drunk-spread-across-social-media/.

35. Greg Sargent, "Why Fox News Thinks the 'Cognitive Decline' Attack on Biden Will Work," *The Washington Post,* June 30, 2020, https:// www.washingtonpost.com/opinions/2020/06/30/why-fox-news-thinks -cognitive-decline-attack-biden-will-work/.

36. David Choi, "In Stunning Reversal, Trump's Personal Doctor Says Trump Dictated a Letter Declaring He Was in 'Astonishingly Excellent' Health during the 2016 Election," *Business Insider*, May 1, 2018, https://www .businessinsider.com/trump-doctor-health-letter-who-wrote-it-2018-5.

3. #ADAPTandRESIST

MY FIRST TWO CHAPTERS focused on illness politics as a tactic of electoral politics used to discredit candidates for political office. I showed how the deployment of the hashtags #SickHillary and #TrumpIsNotWell, and related media and social media coverage, influenced the presidential elections of 2016 and 2020. I now shift my analysis from illness politics as a component of electoral politics and as focused on individuals running for office to an analysis of hashtags used by disability activist groups whose aim is to counter the shame and stigma surrounding illness and disability and create opportunities for sick and disabled people to participate more fully in public life in a variety of ways. As I discussed in the last chapter, for the most part, disability activists have been less interested than nondisabled people in spotlighting Trump's offensive mocking of reporter Serge Kovaleski's disability that was caught on camera in 2015 and replayed frequently during and since the 2016 presidential election campaign. Trump's crass and childish mockery is clearly a sign of a serious case of ableism, long indicated by his disdain for what he perceives as physical and/or emotional weakness. But it is also clear that the constant circulation of this image keeps the focus on Trump and his character and thus functions as a kind of paternalism rather than as a way of increasing the participation of disabled people in the public sphere and creating more accessible, inclusive, and just societies through political activism.

In his essay "Compulsory Able-Bodiedness and Queer/Disabled Existence," queer crip theorist Robert McRuer adapts Adrienne Rich's concept of compulsory heterosexuality to disabled experience, noting the "imbricated systems" of heterosexuality, patriarchy, and able-bodiedness.[1] In his analysis, McRuer makes an important distinction between a "virtually disabled identity," which suggests the inevitability of disabled existence for anyone who lives long enough, and a "critically disabled identity," which demands "access to a newly imagined and newly configured public sphere where full participation is not contingent on an able body."[2] In the final turn in his argument, McRuer considers expressions of "fabulousness" and "severeness" as two modes of criticality used by queer and disabled activists and scholars. According to McRuer, fabulousness is associated with a disarming over-the-top campiness that uses humor as a way of critiquing the status quo, while severity generates "a fierce critique, a defiant critique, one that thoroughly and carefully reads a situation—and I mean reading in the street sense of loudly calling out the inadequacies of a given situation, person, text, or ideology."[3] McRuer mentions several examples of these sorts of in-your-face tactics of illness and disability politics, including Audre Lorde's "army of one-breasted women" that she imagined marching on the U.S. Capitol in *The Cancer Journals* (1980); the Rolling Quads, a coalition of quadriplegic students at the University of California at Berkeley in the late 1960s, who became prominent leaders of the Independent Living Movement; the Deaf Prez Now protests at Gallaudet University in 1988; and ACT UP's nonviolent takeover of the U.S. Food and Drug Administration, also in 1988.[4]

1. Robert McRuer, "Compulsory Able-Bodiedness and Queer/Disabled Existence," in *The Disability Studies Reader*, 3rd ed., ed. Lennard J. Davis, 383–92 (New York: Routledge, 2010), 383–84.

2. McRuer, 388.

3. McRuer, 388.

4. McRuer, 389. For more on McRuer's examples of severely disabled activism, see Lorde, *The Cancer Journals*; Truc Nguyen, "31 Years Ago, Berkeley Disability Activists Sparked a National Movement," KALW Public

In this chapter, I discuss a more recent example of the enactment of a severe disability politics articulated in the series of protests under the hashtag #ADAPTandRESIST in 2017 that were organized by ADAPT, a grassroots disability rights and justice organization known for its nonviolent direct-action tactics.

Returning one last time to the image of Trump's mockery of a disabled person in 2015, for veteran disability activists, including those in ADAPT, the problem is not so much the mockery itself but that such ableist attitudes lead to actions to undo policies and laws that support the rights and needs of disabled people. Thus, as Republicans attempted to repeal and replace the Affordable Care Act and cut and cap Medicaid, ADAPT led numerous protests in Washington, D.C., and elsewhere. These protests in summer 2017 garnered mainstream and social media attention, as images of police removing activists in wheelchairs from Senate Majority Leader Mitch McConnell's office circulated widely. Other images showed police separating ADAPT activists from their wheelchairs to remove and arrest them. Such images of the use of force against a vulnerable population helped drive home ADAPT's message that these policies are a matter of life and death for some people. As one sign at the Capitol proclaimed, "Medicaid is life" for many people with disabilities. Activists like Stephanie Woodward, Gregg Beratan, and Anita Cameron put their vulnerable bodies on the line to generate media coverage and attention on social media about what is at stake—in the most material terms—in the ongoing debates about healthcare in America. The spectacle of ADAPT's direct-action politics created a severe criticality and enacted a highly visible disabled counter-public that punctured ableist attitudes about disability, care, access, and freedom.

Media, TUC Radio, April 5, 2017, https://www.kalw.org/news/2017-04-05/berkeley-disability-activists-took-cues-from-the-civil-rights-era-and-sparked-a-national-movement; Oliver Sacks, *Seeing Voices: A Journey into the World of the Deaf* (New York: Vintage, 1989); and Douglas Crimp and Adam Rolston, *AIDS Demo Graphics* (Seattle: Bay Press, 1990).

Images from the protest at Senate Majority Leader McConnell's office on June 22, 2017, show why direct-action tactics are effective in confronting injustice and raising awareness about issues that might otherwise go unnoticed by people who believe they are unaffected by such politics. In a first-person account of the protests for *Vox*, Stephanie Woodward, the director of advocacy at the Center for Disability Rights in Rochester, New York, and an organizer with ADAPT, opens with surprise that a photograph of her in handcuffs after her arrest on Capitol Hill had gone viral. The photo by fellow disability rights activist Colleen Flanagan is of Woodward from behind sitting in her pink manual wheelchair with her hands cuffed with zip ties behind her wheelchair. This was one of many still photographs and videos of Woodward and other disabled activists that went viral that day.[5] In the essay in *Vox*, Woodward moves from the viral image of her after her arrest to explain some of the decision-making about the protest, and to make a point about the multiple temporalities of activism: "I've been an activist with the Disability Rights group ADAPT for 10 years. When we learned that the Senate planned to vote on a bill that included $800 billion in Medicaid cuts, we knew that we needed to take action quickly. Our months of trying to talk with legislators did not work. We needed to do something more drastic."[6] In this brief account of the process by which she and other activists decided to protest at Senate Majority Leader McConnell's office on Capitol Hill, we learn that Woodward is an experienced activist and that she and ADAPT had first tried less drastic tactics over a longer period. Much of the coverage of the protest at McConnell's office described it as a "sit-in," but according to Woodward, it was meant to be a die-in, "where

5. Colleen Flanagan, June 22, 2017, 1:26 pm, http://twitter.com /ColleenFlanagan.

6. Stephanie Woodward, "I Was Pulled Out of My Wheelchair by Police. It Could Be Worse. Trumpcare Could Pass," *Vox*, June 28, 2017, https://www.vox.com/first-person/2017/6/27/15876442/healthcare -medicaid-cuts-disability-protests.

protestors physically disrupt a space by laying down their bodies to simulate corpses" to represent "the harm that the bill would do to so many disabled people."[7] Die-ins date back to at least the 1960s when antiwar and environmental activists used them to highlight the effects of both mass destruction from war and slow death from climate change.[8] In the 1980s, AIDS activist groups like ACT UP used die-ins to demonstrate the horror of AIDS, as well as the U.S. government's lack of concerted and caring response to the spread of the disease because it was initially perceived as a "gay disease." As I will show below, dying-in was not a new tactic for ADAPT.

Colleen Flanagan shared the photo of Woodward handcuffed in her wheelchair with a tweet that said, "Medicaid is important to disabled people. We raise our voice and get answered with handcuffs. #ADAPTandRESIST."[9] Flanagan's snapshot shows the aftermath of the protest, not #ADAPTandRESIST in action. Yet many other images of Woodward show her while protesting and raising her voice, and these would also go viral. It's not difficult to see why. Woodward is a petite white woman with a striking mane of curly red hair. On the day of the protest, she wore a pair of bright pink sunglasses that matched the color of her wheelchair, and in several of the images of her participating in the protest, the sunglasses are on her head rather stylishly holding back her hair. She had also painted her nails with bright pink nail polish, creating an ensemble of accessories matching her flashy pink wheelchair. In a photograph taken by AP photographer Jacquelyn Martin that also went viral, Woodward has been separated from her wheelchair and is being carried by at least three much burlier Capitol police officers (Figure 3). In Martin's photograph, Woodward is literally

7. Woodward, "I Was Pulled Out of My Wheelchair by Police."

8. For an interesting historical analysis of the die-in as political tactic, see Daniel Ross, "The Die-In: A Short History," *Active History*, June 29, 2015, https://activehistory.ca/2015/06/the-die-in/.

9. Colleen Flanagan, June 22, 2017, 1:26 pm, http://twitter.com /ColleenFlanagan.

engulfed by the bodies of the police officers, and we only see her head and one outstretched arm. She is captured looking terrified with her eyes turned back toward the camera, as if looking for and appealing to us, the viewers of the photograph and, more generally, the American people who may or may not understand what the protest is about. Her mouth is wide open, shouting. Her arm reaches out from her body, in a theatrical pose, imploring us viewers, as if to also say, "please, help me."

Martin's photograph powerfully captures Woodward in action, passively resisting the police in an act of civil disobedience. As she explains in her *Vox* piece, she knew what she was doing in relation to the law: "I did nothing to insult or instigate the cops, but I refused to comply with the police's orders to get out of the office."[10] As activists understand, refusing to comply creates a dramatic scene in which the state confronts an immovable object—the body of the protester. If the still photograph captures Woodward beseeching us to care about her cause, video of Woodward being removed shows a harrowing and dramatic scene of the state using disproportionate and excessive force against a disabled person. We see her being lifted out of her wheelchair by three police officers, and as this is happening, she never stops screaming one of the chants used by protestors, "No cuts to Medicaid."[11] In some videos of the incident, we can see that, as she is being lifted, her black t-shirt rides up her torso, exposing her midriff and highlighting further her vulnerability and violation. In a video report on the protests for the *Washington Post,* Woodward says in an interview, "We're here fighting for Medicaid for millions of people with disabilities who rely on Medicaid. Without it we will die. There are huge cuts to Medicaid which will result in people with disabilities being forced into nursing facilities and ultimately dying there. And quite frank-

10. Woodward, "I Was Pulled Out of My Wheelchair by Police."
11. "Protesters Block Hallway outside McConnell's Office," *Washington Post*, June 22, 2017, https://youtu.be/rBBb997LlDU.

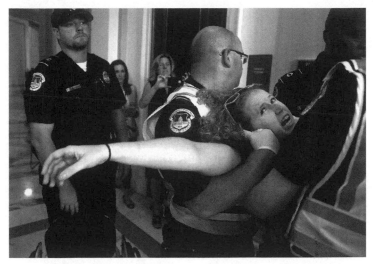

Figure 3. Capitol police remove disability activist Stephanie Woodward, of Rochester, New York, from a die-in organized by ADAPT at Senate Majority Leader Mitch McConnell's office on June 22, 2017. Woodward and other activists were arrested as they protested Republican lawmakers' attempts to repeal the Affordable Care Act and cap funding for Medicaid. AP Photo/Jacquelyn Martin. https://www .vox.com/first-person/2017/6/27/15876442/healthcare-medicaid-cuts-disability -protests. Reprinted with permission AP Photo/Jacquelyn Martin.

ly, I'd rather go to jail than die."[12] Other activists, including Susan Stahl and Rhoda Gibson, are also interviewed by the *Washington Post,* and, like Woodward, they emphasize that, thanks to Medicaid, they are able to live independently in the community rather than be institutionalized. ADAPT's direct-action tactics create a spectacle of state power confronting vulnerable disabled people who simply want to be able to continue to live independently. Another ADAPT activist Julie Farrar links the #ADAPTandRESIST protests to earlier activism for disability rights, asserting, "This is really a life-and-death matter and I have not been this terrified in a very long

12. "Protesters Block Hallway outside McConnell's Office."

time."[13] Farrar adds that twenty-seven years ago she was "crawling up the steps to the Capitol to get the Americans with Disabilities Act passed," emphasizing both the *longue durée* of struggle for disability rights in the United States and that disabled activists have been and continue to be at the center of that struggle.

The reference to the Capitol Crawl, which took place in 1990 and was also organized by ADAPT, indicates an understanding of the importance of creating images of struggle for the media that will get the attention of the American people more widely.[14] Like the Capitol Crawl, this was illness politics in action confronting an uncaring state, and images of what was at stake in this confrontation circulated widely in the media and on social media through the hashtag #ADAPTandRESIST. This was a savvy strategy by activists to use the media to generate empathy for their determination to stop the cuts to Medicaid funding that allows them to remain in community. This was a political demonstration in its most classic sense: as a public showing of feeling about what is at stake regarding a particular issue.

The protests on Capitol Hill were just one of many demonstrations organized by ADAPT in what they called the #SummerOfADAPT.

---

13. "Protesters Block Hallway outside McConnell's Office."

14. For a fascinating account of the Capitol Crawl, see Mike Erwin, "An Oral History of the Capitol Crawl," *New Mobility*, July 1, 2020, https://newmobility.com/the-capitol-crawl/, which also demonstrates the multiple temporalities and spaces of activism. Bob Kafka, one of the national organizers for ADAPT who helped plan the Capitol Crawl, describes the rationale for the action this way: "The system people [disability advocacy lobbyists] were stalled. The ADA had gotten stuck in the House of Representatives, and they were not able to get it moving again. We wanted to show that 'access is a civil right' is more than just words, that we were willing to take action. We wanted to make sure the statement we made was symbolic and visual." Julie Farrar, who was nineteen at the time, recalls of the action, "The feeling of camaraderie was palpable—the excitement on our march there, the staging. I don't remember the speeches. I just remember feeling so proud in a very sacred communal way of being a part of it all." And Anita Cameron, another longtime ADAPT activist whom I discuss further below, noted, "I felt that we were crawling our way into the history books."

As senators went home for the July 4th recess, ADAPT activists across the country sought to communicate directly to GOP senators in their home states about the devastating impact on their lives that a cut in Medicaid would bring. In Denver, activists conducted a sit-in at Senator Cory Gardner's office for fifty-eight hours to tell the senator their concerns. As in the protest on Capitol Hill in Washington, D.C., activists sought to communicate the crucial fact that without continued support from Medicaid, they could not live independently in the community. Senator Gardner never met with the activists, and they were eventually arrested and removed from his office. Activist Carrie Ann Lucas was charged with trespassing and because she refused to help police operate her motorized wheelchair, she was also charged with interference. As she explained in an interview, echoing Woodward's comments at the time of her arrest in Washington, D.C., "While I would not resist arrest, I was not willing to help the police."[15] Lucas's noncooperation fits into a long history of nonviolent civil disobedience as embodied form of resistance. In this case, her power chair is not an instrument used by her body but part of her body that went limp as the police tried to remove her. Her careful distinction between resisting arrest and refusing to help police is not only semantic; it is also tactical, indicating someone trained to do this kind of activism.

The Longer History of Direct-Action Illness Politics

As I've already indicated, ADAPT and its direct-action political tactics are not new. While some commentators in 2017 made links between ADAPT and ACT UP, these accounts often mistakenly credited ACT UP as an influence on ADAPT, but ADAPT pre-dates

15. Erica Meltzer, "Activist Carrie Ann Lucas Told Denver Police to Google How to Use Her Wheelchair; Now She's Charged with Interference," *Denverite*, June 30, 2017, https://denverite.com/2017/06 /30/refusing-tell-officers-operate-wheelchair-activist-carrie-ann-lucas -charged-interference/.

ACT UP by at least a decade. Taking a longer view of health activism and illness politics as I do in my work suggests ACT UP is not the original source of health activism but a link between earlier health-activist movements, including those associated with the women's liberation movement, Civil Rights groups like the Black Panther Party and the Young Lords, anti-psychiatry, and environmental justice movements.[16] This longer view would also include the Independent Living Movement (ILM), which has advocated since the early 1970s for disabled people to live in their communities and not in nursing homes or other institutions, to make decisions about their own lives and care, and in general articulates an everyday ethics of self-determination.

The ILM emerged from the activist milieu centered around Berkeley in the late 1960s and early 1970s, but the movement quickly spread beyond Berkeley to other less countercultural milieus. The second Independent Living Center was the Atlantis Community founded by the Reverend Wade Blank in Denver in 1975. ADAPT emerged out of this local Denver disability-activist environment that Atlantis cultivated and the group first garnered widespread media coverage in 1978 for protests calling for wheelchair-accessible public transportation.[17] In July 1978, some thirty disabled protestors in wheelchairs surrounded two Denver Regional Transportation District (RTD) buses, preventing them from moving, to draw attention to the fact that the RTD did not provide transportation for people with disabilities. As the *Denver Post* reported, "A major traffic jam and three arrests resulted."[18]

16. This is one of the key arguments of my book *Indirect Action: Schizophrenia, Epilepsy, AIDS, and the Course of Health Activism* (Minneapolis: University of Minnesota Press, 2016), which looks at what I call the prehistory of AIDS activism.

17. The *Denver Post* had a special feature on the origins of ADAPT in Denver at the time of the protests against repeal of the ACA in summer 2017: Danika Worthington, "Meet the Disabled Activists from Denver Who Changed a Nation," *Denver Post*, July 5, 2017, https://www.denverpost.com /2017/07/05/adapt-disabled-activists-denver/.

18. Worthington.

One photograph from the protest in 1978 shows four disabled activists asleep in the street in front of a bus, preventing the bus from moving. Barricades can be seen in the background of the photo, blocking the street. An empty wheelchair is also in the middle of the street with what appears to be a sign propped on its seat. Signs have also been placed on the large front window screen of the bus, creatively held in place by the bus's windshield wipers, as if the bus has been commandeered to support the activists' cause. One sign has two simple equations: an ambulatory stick figure with "= Free Ride" next to it above a figure of a wheelchair user with "= No Ride" next to it. The other sign has the same symbol for a wheelchair user next to the words "TAXATION WITHOUT TRANSPORTATION." Looking back at earlier protests, we can see that, as with the #ADAPTandRESIST actions in 2017, one goal is to create a visually compelling narrative of determination in the face of adversity. As the caption to the photograph mentions, the four demonstrators sleeping in the street were part of a group of thirty disabled protestors "who maintained an overnight vigil to dramatize the need for greater accessibility to public transportation for the disabled."[19]

The ADAPT acronym initially stood for American Disabled for Accessible Public Transport. As the political issues the group has engaged in have broadened, ADAPT would maintain the acronym but adapt—or, in the language of disability theory and practice today, we might say, "crip"—its meaning. Now ADAPT stands for American Disabled for Attendant Programs Today. The fluid meanings of the acronym reflect the importance of both freedom of movement in the public sphere and access to good care and assistance in both the public and private sphere as necessary to enable full citizenship and participation of disabled people. The ADAPT activists know much is at stake in the battle over health care. For these activists, illness and disability are material conditions of everyday life that require

19. Worthington.

creative responses at the level of both the individual and society. They challenge us to adapt—not simply our bodies and ourselves but our society—so that everyone can fully participate in political and social life.

After the #SummerOfADAPT

Protests did not end at the end of the #SummerOfADAPT. In March 2018, hoping to draw on momentum from the summer before, members of ADAPT gathered again in D.C., this time camping outside the home of FDA Director Scott Gottlieb for over a week in cold and rain before targeting the FDA offices in a protest to stop aversive electroshock "treatments" at the Judge Rotenberg Center in Massachusetts. The ADAPTers were steadfast in their commitment to confront Gottlieb and convince him to take action to stop what they assert is not treatment but torture of disabled people. In press releases about this action, ADAPT emphasized the strength and perseverance of its members, who endured physical hardships and risked arrest to bring attention to injustice.[20] They created an encampment near Gottlieb's home, which they dubbed "ADAPT Freedom Park," targeting a public figure who had the power to make positive change for institutionalized people and drawing attention more widely to the horror of aversive treatments. While the FDA protests generated less mainstream media coverage than the spectacle of disabled people being physically removed by police from the halls of Congress, ADAPT understands that the fight for the rights and needs of disabled people must operate in many registers at once. ADAPTers like Anita Cameron, who has been arrested more than 130 times in the fight for disability rights, are savvy activists, using the tactics of direct action to bring into the public domain

20. John Zangas, "'Stop the Shock': FDA Director's Home Beseiged [*sic*] by Disability Rights Activists," adapt.org, March 22, 2018, https://adapt .org/stop-the-shock-fda-directors-home-beseiged-by-disability-rights -activists/.

the cruel and otherwise unseen "treatments" of highly vulnerable institutionalized people.[21] The tactic of disability as spectacle is deployed to shame the nondisabled to contemplate the vulnerability of institutionalized people. #ADAPTandRESIST is democracy in action around the question of what kind of society we want—one that would enable the many to flourish and live valuable lives, or one that protects and enables the few.

As a campaign, #ADAPTandRESIST cultivated a heroic activist image of both individual commitment and collective solidarity through the spatio-temporal politics of direct action. They turned ableist assumptions about disabled people into an advantage. Indeed, I would argue that there is a performative vulnerability at work in these protests. To describe as performative the vulnerability of ADAPT's direct action politics does not mean that I don't think disabled activists are not actually vulnerable when they do this kind of activism. My work explores illness as performative, "performative" understood here through the lens of both social interactionist theories, which explore the constitution of the self in the practices of everyday life,[22] and speech act theories of performative utterances, which explore how saying can be doing.[23] We can see how diagnosis in particular is a performative utterance; doctors have the capacity to make someone ill or not, by declaring them so. As I will

21. For an analysis of the multiple sites and practices of confinement, and the importance of disability critique in relation to carceral studies and prison activism, see Liat Ben-Moshe, Chris Chapman, and Allison C. Carey, eds. *Disability Incarcerated: Imprisonment and Disability in the United States and Canada* (New York: Palgrave Macmillan, 2014).

22. See, for example, Erving Goffman, *The Presentation of Self in Everyday Life* (New York: Anchor, 1959), and *Stigma*.

23. I am referring to the work first articulated by J. L. Austin in *How to Do Things with Words* (Cambridge, Mass.: Harvard University Press, 1961), and later expanded by Jacques Derrida, *Margins of Philosophy*, trans. Alan Bass (Chicago: University of Chicago Press, 1982); Judith Butler, *Excitable Speech: A Politics of the Performative* (New York: Routledge, 1997); and Eve Kosofsky Sedgwick, *Touching Feeling: Affect, Pedagogy, Performativity* (Durham, N.C.: Duke University Press, 2003); among others.

discuss further in chapters 5 and 6, as is often the case with emergent and not fully understood illnesses like ME/CFS and long Covid,
a person may be deemed not ill or, sometimes, mentally rather than
physically ill. Yet here I am also interested in how doing illness
and disability *politics* performs illness in various ways. In the case
of #ADAPTandRESIST, activists do illness and disability in public
combining a rhetoric and politics of vulnerability and heroism while
also making disability community visible to others, disabled and
nondisabled. Being seen fighting for their rights, as well as for the
rights of others, confers agency on a population often perceived
as lacking agency. Put simply, this is an effective affective politics.

Postscripts to #ADAPTandRESIST

I want to close this chapter by offering two brief postscripts about
ADAPT's #ADAPTandRESIST campaign, which demonstrate what
is at stake in illness and disability politics at individual and structural levels: the first is the tragic death of Carrie Ann Lucas in 2019,
and the second, accusations of racism and xenophobia against one
of ADAPT's leaders, Bruce Darling, and statements disavowing
Darling's words and actions by the NCIL and ADAPT.

Less than two years after Carrie Ann Lucas was arrested in
Denver, she tragically passed away, on February 24, 2019, at the
age of only forty-seven. In a post on her Facebook page announcing her death, Lucas's family and friends stated that she "died after
an arbitrary denial from an insurance company caused a plethora
of health problems, exacerbating her disabilities and eventually
leading to her premature death."[24] In an obituary in *Forbes* with
the headline, "You Probably Haven't Heard of Her and That's a
Problem," Sarah Kim quoted from the family's assessment that

24. Quoted in Sarah Kim, "Carrie Ann Lucas Dies at Age 47. You
Probably Haven't Heard of Her and That's a Problem," *Forbes*, February 25,
2019, https://www.forbes.com/sites/sarahkim/2019/02/25/carrie-ann-lucas
-dies/?sh=5323e6eb119e.

terrible decisions led directly to Lucas's premature death, and she asserted more generally that "discussions surrounding disability rights issues are still kept in secrecy."[25] Kim also addressed the problem of disability representation, noting that, "when disability is represented in the media, it is mostly through the lenses of pity or inspiration—never through a human rights perspective. Most of the featured stories are about someone overcoming the odds despite having a disability."[26] Kim goes on to chronicle and celebrate Lucas's activist work, ending her tribute by quoting further from the Facebook post that calls on all of us to fight the inhumane and deadly decisions that deem some lives not worthy of the cost of care: "For all intents and purposes, a shero of our community was murdered in the name of cost containment. This is why we MUST fight those measures with all we have."[27]

Even as Lucas's loved ones and fellow activists honored her life work by calling for a continuation of the fight for justice by and for disabled people, there were some obituaries that fell into the trap of the overcoming narrative, even as they sought to acknowledge the gravity of the loss of such a powerful figure in the disability community. In a long obituary for the *New York Times,* for example, Katharine Q. Seelye lauds Lucas as a champion for people, and especially parents, with disabilities, and mentions her arrest on "charges of trespassing after a 58-hour sit-in at the Denver office of Senator Cory Gardner."[28] Seelye notes that Lucas and other activists were arrested "protesting the Republican plan to repeal the Affordable Care Act, which would have reduced Medicaid funding and eliminated services that make it possible for people with disabilities to live independently."[29] Yet, despite close attention to

25. Kim.

26. Kim.

27. Kim, emphasis in original.

28. Katharine Q. Seelye, "Carrie Ann Lucas, Champion for Disabled Parents, Dies at 47," *The New York Times*, February 27, 2019, https://www.nytimes.com/2019/02/27/obituaries/carrie-ann-lucas-dead.html.

29. Seelye.

Lucas's activism, Seelye's obituary describes the cause of Lucas's death simply as "complications of septic shock," not mentioning the insurance company's denial of a specific drug—an inhalable antibiotic—that was needed to treat her condition nor her family's insistence that her death was preventable.[30] Seelye's obituary does precisely what Kim cautions against: focusing on Lucas's activism as a form of individual overcoming rather than on the structural ableism of a failed health-care system that she protested against and that caused her death.

Finally, in another upsetting postscript to #ADAPTandRESIST, I want to briefly mention the controversy surrounding comments made in the summer of 2019 by Bruce Darling, a long-time leader of ADAPT and at that time President of the Board of the National Council on Independent Living (NCIL). Darling and other ADAPT activists were meeting with Anna Eshoo, a Democratic member of Congress from California. In a tweet thread on July 16, 2019, Cal Montgomery, a member of ADAPT who was at the meeting, calls out Darling, who he says made it clear he was representing both ADAPT and NCIL when he made negative comments about immigrants in the meeting.[31] Montgomery links to a video posted on Facebook of the meeting and draws viewers' attention to the point at about the 14-minute mark in the video where Darling expresses what he says is "our talking point." Montgomery quotes Darling in full over three tweets in the thread saying the following:

> "Our talking point is, 'Democrats care more about people who are not legally in this country than their own citizens who are disabled.' It really is what the message is here. That basically [pointing to different disabled activists] you and you and you and you, you are less than. You are not worthy. We are more concerned about immigrants who happened to come here in a non-legal manner than we are with our own citizens, and we will lock disabled people up. This is going

30. Seelye.

31. Cal Montgomery, July 16, 2019, 2:44 pm, https://twitter.com/Cal _Montgomery/.

to be the message from the dais at the [National Council on Independent Living] conference. This is not what Democrats want. It's not what we want."[32]

Montgomery's next tweet in the thread emphatically distances himself from Darling's remarks, noting that Darling does not speak for him: "Let me be clear. Nobody has my consent to use my name, my experience, my trauma, my commitment to disability rights or my work to suggest that disabled people with and without citizenship are in a competition for justice. He's speaking on my behalf without my consent."[33] Montgomery's tweet thread circulated widely, and other disability activists spoke out against what they saw as the racism and xenophobia behind Darling's comments, as well as a casual assumption about the whiteness of the disability community. Disabled activist Alice Wong, one of the founders of #CripTheVote, which I will discuss in the next chapter, created a wakelet to document responses to Darling's comments under the heading "Racism, immigration, and the disability community: A snapshot."[34] The next day, Darling offered an apology of sorts on Twitter, taking sole responsibility for his comments and clarifying that he was not speaking on behalf of ADAPT or NCIL, which he noted are both "working hard to advance intersectional justice."[35]

Later the same day, the board of directors of the NCIL published a statement saying they had unanimously accepted Darling's resignation and that they "unequivocally denounce" his statements.[36]

32. Cal Montgomery, July 16, 2019, 2:44 pm, https://twitter.com/Cal_Montgomery/.

33. Cal Montgomery, July 16, 2019, 2:44 pm, https://twitter.com/Cal_Montgomery/.

34. Alice Wong, "Racism, immigration, and the disability community: A snapshot," wakelet, @AliceWong9697, https://wakelet.com/wake/e7d48cb7-7ea8-42a4-8bb7-078cb796ebc7.

35. Bruce Darling, July 17, 2019, 12:31 am, https://twitter.com/ADAPTerBruce/.

36. "Statement from NCIL's Board of Directors," *The Advocacy Monitor: Independent Living News & Policy from the National Council on*

In their statement, the NCIL took the opportunity to show how immigration and detention are disability-justice issues for a variety of reasons, including because disabled people are among those detained at the border and seeking asylum and because the conditions in the camps "are resulting in detainees acquiring trauma-related disabilities." They also condemned rhetoric that sought "to pit the disability community against those who are seeking asylum in the U.S." and sent a strong message of solidarity with detainees and those seeking to immigrate to the United States.[37] Finally, the NCIL board acknowledged that the Independent Living Movement could have better representation in its leadership of multiply marginalized people and promised to devote significant time at the upcoming conference mentioned by Darling in his comments on how to make the ILM more inclusive.

ADAPT, too, denounced Darling immediately, beginning with a statement of "REAL Values and Commitment" signed by several ADAPT chapters in the week following Darling's comments.[38] The statement began:

> We take responsibility and apologize for the hurtful and damaging actions that have taken place under ADAPT's name. There is no excuse. It is wholly unacceptable for ADAPT leaders to pit other groups fighting for freedom against one another—no one is free until we all are free. The ADAPT Chapters cosigning this statement are dedicated to changing the way ADAPT is currently operating on a National level, how we address racist, ableist, nationalist, homophobic, transphobic, sexist, classist, and all hate speech within our ADAPT community, and get back on the path of direct action grassroots community organizing to Free All People.[39]

Independent Living, July 17, 2019, https://advocacymonitor.com/statement-from-ncils-board-of-directors/.

37. "Statement from NCIL's Board of Directors."

38. "ADAPT's Statement of REAL Values and Commitment," adapt.org, no date, https://adapt.org/adapts-statement-of-real-values-and-commitment/.

39. "ADAPT's Statement of REAL Values and Commitment."

Eventually, in a brief statement released on February 17, 2020, ADAPT disavowed Bruce Darling. Signed by the ADAPT Collective, the statement read in full: "It is clear that, for some time now, Bruce Darling has not been acting in the best interests of ADAPT. Bruce Darling no longer represents, or speaks for National ADAPT. Bruce Darling no longer is an organizer or leader for National ADAPT."[40] For me, this is not so much the story of one activist who was canceled but is an example of illness and disability politics in action in the form of reflection on the leadership and decision-making of the group, as well as on the overall framing of the issues and the tactics and strategies deployed by the group. As I will discuss in the next two chapters, the heroic image of protest in the form of direct-action civil disobedience in public spaces that ADAPT utilized to good effect in its #ADAPTandRESIST campaign is not the only model of disability and illness politics in action. With #CripTheVote, we move from the spaces of political power in the United States (the U.S. Capitol and senators' offices in Washington, D.C., and at home) to virtual spaces of a becoming-disability-community.

40. "National ADAPT Statement Disavowing Bruce Darling," February 17, 2020, https://nationaladapt.org/national-adapt-statement-disavowing -bruce-darling/.

4. #CripTheVote

IN THIS CHAPTER, I turn to how disability activists have sought to challenge—or "crip"—the commonplace image of the figure of the activist in the streets protesting loudly and proudly, defiant, and disobedient. Conceptually and in practice, #CripTheVote provides a counterimage to the disabled activist in the public square or in the halls of Congress, as we saw in the last chapter. #CripTheVote began as a hashtag and has operated solely as an online campaign, primarily using Twitter to organize chats on a wide range of disability-related issues. Like ADAPT, #CripTheVote is interested in creating the conditions of possibility for the participation of disabled people in public life, but via online not in-person modalities of participation and protest. Created by Gregg Beratan (himself a member of ADAPT, who was arrested on Capitol Hill during the #SummerOfADAPT, and a policy analyst for the Center for Disability Rights), Andrew Pulrang (an Independent Living Movement advocate and disability blogger), and Alice Wong (a writer, activist, and the creator of the Disability Visibility blog and podcast) in the run-up to the 2016 presidential election, #CripTheVote's mission statement explains that it "is a nonpartisan campaign to engage both voters and politicians in a productive discussion about disability issues in the United States with the hope that disability takes on greater prominence within the

American political landscape."[1] I begin this chapter by discussing a conversation between the three founders of #CripTheVote in 2017 that took place just after the protests led by ADAPT at the U.S. Capitol and statehouses across the country, and in which they reflect on both the #SummerOfADAPT and #CripTheVote. I then go back to the founding of the group and their work around the 2016 election before looking at how they sustained the project through the 2020 election and beyond. I contend that #CripTheVote has had a significant impact on the increasing visibility of disability issues in electoral politics, as well as on more widespread knowledge about and critique of ableism and stigma associated with disability in U.S. politics and culture.[2] I write this in the immediate aftermath of John Fetterman's 2022 win over Mehmet Oz in the race for Senate in Pennsylvania, despite Fetterman having had a serious stroke after winning the Democratic party nomination. In a debate only weeks before the election, Fetterman used closed captioning as an accommodation for auditory processing issues resulting from the stroke. Thus, disability and access have been in the news, and although much of the coverage of Fetterman's attempt to run for office while recovering from stroke has been ableist, there has also been an important analysis of and counternarrative to that ableism. I think the influence of #CripTheVote has generated a more nuanced and widespread understanding of how ableism operates, and how it can be counteracted, in poli-

1. "About #CripTheVote," Disability Visibility Project blog, November 10, 2016. https://disabilityvisibilityproject.com/2016/11/10/1110 -post-election-cripthevote-chat-whatsnext/.

2. In showcasing #CripTheVote in this chapter, I will also frequently draw on Alice Wong's linked but also separate work as creator of the *Disability Visibility* website and podcast. Wong's website has been used to promote and archive #CripTheVote Twitter chats and other activities. Wong and others use the hashtag #DisabilityVisibility and, along with her personal Twitter account (@SFdirewolf), Wong also tweets as @ DisVisibility, an account for "creating, amplifying & sharing disability media and culture," as the bio for the account notes.

tics. I don't think it's an exaggeration to say that by raising issues of ableism and access in relation to participation in political and social life in the United States, #CripTheVote had an at least indirect hand in Fetterman's win despite, or perhaps because of, many pundits' clearly ableist discomfort with Fetterman's debate performance.

"The Revolution Is Here"

In the first episode of her *Disability Visibility* podcast in 2017, recorded in July, "days after the GOP health care bill died in the Senate," Wong interviewed Beratan and Pulrang on "Activism and Disability Community," and they reflected on the #SummerOfADAPT protests as well as on their ongoing work as the founders and coorganizers of the #CripTheVote campaign. Wong introduced the conversation by providing a somewhat unconventional image of revolutionary activism as happening online: "The revolution is here," Wong quipped. "One podcast, one transcript, one tweet at a time."[3] The three begin the conversation by discussing the activism that had taken place over the past year to prevent the Republican plan to repeal and replace the Affordable Care Act, activism that culminated in the #SummerOfADAPT. Wong describes the "great awakening" that took place through these protests, as nondisabled people gained a "little sense of what Medicaid is, what it does, and just how many

3. The podcast and transcript are available on the *Disability Visibility* website: Alice Wong with Gregg Beratan and Andrew Pulrang, "Activism and Disability Community," *Disability Visibility Podcast*, Episode 1, September 13, 2017, https://disabilityvisibilityproject.com/2017/09/13/disability-visibility-podcast-ep-1-activism-and-the-disability-community/. Wong continued hosting the *Disability Visibility* podcast until April 2021, ending with podcast #100. This conversation, as well as another conversation between the three founders of #CripTheVote, are also included together in a condensed and edited form in Wong's memoir *Year of the Tiger: An Activist's Life* (New York: Vintage, 2022), 73. Some citations will be from the condensed interview in *Year of the Tiger* and some from the longer version on the podcast.

people it touches."[4] Beratan adds, "I think one of the heartening things has been seeing people realize what value Medicaid adds to our society, that people are able to work and live and raise their families, go to school, give birth to healthy kids, because of what Medicaid provides."[5] The three then discuss the need for a variety of political tactics, including direct action as a "kind of secret weapon," as Wong puts it.[6] Pulrang expresses appreciation that disability activism has been "really focused and disciplined on issues and their actual effects rather than . . . going along with the obsession with Trump . . . Trump the man, Trump the weirdo."[7] It is this comment from Pulrang about Trump that then shifts the discussion from #SummerOfADAPT to #CripTheVote.

The three acknowledge that this focus on broader issues and not a "cult of personality" surrounding any one politician, or as devolving into "partisan crap," explains the group's effectiveness in bringing disability into political conversations in the United States and beyond. Pulrang explains that the purpose of #CripTheVote was not to approach "disability as a fairly simple and narrow range of issues" but as "something that relates to a huge tent of issues."[8] And Wong points out that, although the group was initially planning to disband after the 2016 presidential election, they decided to keep going as a way to continue building the community that had emerged and grown out of the hashtag and Twitter chats.

By creating virtual spaces in which disabled people and their allies can engage with issues and build community, #CripTheVote's tactics are different from ADAPT's, but no less important as a modality for and means of access to political participation for disabled people. The group has explicitly challenged the ableism of the fre-

---

4. Wong, *Year of the Tiger*, 74.

5. Wong, 75.

6. Wong with Beratan and Pulrang, "Activism and Disability Community."

7. Wong with Beratan and Pulrang.

8. Wong with Beratan and Pulrang.

quently voiced critique that dismisses "hashtag activism" as not real activism, articulating instead for the importance of diverse forms of engagement and participation. While marching in the streets, occupying public spaces, and getting arrested are often effective activist practices, as shown in the last chapter, the more accretive practices of community building and creating networks of support and mutual aid are equally important, if often less immediately visible and operating in a different, more indirect, temporality to direct-action politics.

Importantly, #CripTheVote has also been concerned with emphasizing the intersectionality of disability experience, both in terms of the many kinds of impairment under the disability umbrella, as well as the many ways race, gender, class, and sexuality inflect and intersect with the multiplicity of disability experiences and vice versa. They have made a space for a wide variety of people to share their disability experiences, as well as for discussion of how white supremacist and cisheteropatriarchal systems function through ableist attitudes and disabling structures. Thus, their work joins recent work in disability studies seeking to, as Jasbir Puar puts it in *The Right to Maim,* "disrupt the normative (white, male, middle-class, physically impaired) subjects that have historically dominated the field."[9] As Puar asserts, "The epistemic whiteness of the field is no dirty secret,"[10] a problem sometimes also reflected in activist work that seeks to distinguish deserving from undeserving recipients of social and political support, as we saw in relation to Bruce Darling's disturbing comments about immigrants in the last chapter.

---

9. Puar, *The Right to Maim,* xix. Puar mentions disability scholars Nirmala Erevelles's *Disability and Difference in Global Contexts: Enabling a Transformative Body Politic* (New York: Palgrave Macmillan, 2011) and Christopher M. Bell's edited volume *Blackness and Disability: Critical Examinations and Cultural Interventions* (East Lansing: Michigan State University Press, 2011) as having "insistently pointed out the need in disability studies for intersectional analysis," xix.

10. Puar, *The Right to Maim,* xix.

The Emergence of #CripTheVote

#CripTheVote held its first Twitter chat before a Democratic Party candidate debate on February 11, 2016, and their second before a Republican Party candidate debate two days later. The group then conducted a survey to find out what disabled people thought were the top policy issues that they wanted candidates for president and other elected offices to address.[11] In March 2016, the group held two more chats on disability and health policy, which incorporated the survey results by organizing the discussions to address the top five areas of concern: healthcare, civil rights and discrimination, employment, accessibility, and housing. After these chats, the three founders began to invite guest hosts as another means to expand the already-burgeoning online community that the hashtag and conversations were fostering. In April 2016, for example, a chat on voter accessibility for and suppression and disenfranchisement of people with disabilities included as one of the guest hosts Carrie Ann Lucas, the activist discussed in the last chapter who was arrested in 2017 with other ADAPTers at Senator Gardner's office in Colorado and who at the time was also executive director of Disabled Parents Rights. This chat asked questions about voter registration, experiences of disabled people at polling places with

11. In the first survey, 508 people responded and the top three disability policy priorities were: health care, civil rights/discrimination, and accessibility. The top three disability policy ideas were: hire and appoint more disabled people to government and policymaking positions, pass the Disability Integration Act to promote independent living instead of nursing homes, and require disability awareness training for law enforcement. In 2018, #CripTheVote conducted its second disability issues survey. They received 589 responses and the top three disability policy priorities were the same as in 2016. The top three disability policy ideas changed from 2016 with "Defend Social Security and Medicaid/Medicare against political attacks" increasing almost 20 percentage points, followed by hire and appoint more disabled people to government and policymaking positions and require disability awareness training for law enforcement. Results of the survey can be found here: http://cripthevote.blogspot.com/p/2016-survey.html.

staff and voting technologies, and about voting rights for institutionalized and intellectually disabled people. Before her untimely death, Lucas was a frequent participant in #CripTheVote chats and had run, unsuccessfully, for Town Board in her hometown of Windsor, Colorado.

In another later chat featuring disabled candidates for office, Lucas answered a question I posed about the difference between activism, specifically direct-action protests, and serving in office. Lucas's thoughtful response referred to the multiple temporalities and spaces of politics: "Direct action is about change," she tweeted. "Governing is often about compromise. One must be an ethical leader when pushed to compromise."[12] This response captures the multilayered approach to disability in action that #CripTheVote makes space and time for. Here we have a statement made by a disabled woman candidate for local office in the United States describing the distinction between direct-action politics and the politics of compromise. This statement is made as part of a chat on Twitter whose purpose is to increase the participation of disabled people in politics, by utilizing other modalities beyond direct action and serving in office to involve people in public life. Without being overly sanguine about social media's transformative potential, what the organizers of #CripTheVote grasped and put into action is the possibility that virtual spaces might increase access to public space and allow for greater participation among people who, for a variety of reasons, find it difficult to negotiate certain spaces at certain times and at certain speeds. This emphasis on creating and sustaining access and connection is a key aspect of disability justice work as a kind of homemaking. In her book about the disability justice performance work of Sins Invalid, Shayda Kafai notes, "we all deserve connection and access to crip-centric liberated zone,"[13]

12. Carrie Ann Lucas, October 12, 2017, 8:39pm, https://twitter.com/DisabilityCubed/status/918622296721408000.

13. Kafai, *Crip Kinship*, 118.

and online activities and programming allows for people to connect with others from home. In this way, Kafai explains, "home becomes an expansive place, hundreds of thousands of miles wide."[14]

In a qualitative content analysis of the #CripTheVote campaign in 2016, social scientist Heather Walker analyzed more than 11,000 tweets with the hashtag to provide a "concentrated look into how disabled people used Twitter as a tool of political engagement in the 2016 United States Presidential election."[15] In examining data from #CripTheVote Twitter chats, Walker did not find that the chats were particularly successful in achieving one of the top stated goals of the #CripTheVote campaign in 2016: "To get disability issues mentioned during the presidential debate cycle."[16] Yet, as Walker notes, while this may be true at face value, she also wanted to think more expansively about what #CripTheVote achieved beyond this very time-specific and limited goal of getting a question about disability into a presidential debate in an election year. Walker argues that what #CripTheVote accomplished instead was to "counter ableist ideologies" and to amplify the lived experiences and personal stories of disabled people. She discusses four counternarratives that emerged through the campaign and hashtag that points to the agency of disabled people despite ableist attitudes and structural violence that constrains agency: "(1) disabled people are politically aware; (2) disabled people have voice; (3) the opinions of disabled people matter; and (4) disabled people will fight for their rights."[17] Walker calls #CripTheVote a "'watershed moment' for contemporary disability studies," an assessment I wholeheartedly agree with. If we extend the analy-

14. Kafai, 118.

15. Heather Walker, "#CripTheVote: How Disabled Activists Used Twitter for Political Engagement during the 2016 Presidential Election," *Participation: Journal of Audience and Reception Studies* 17, no. 1 (May 2020): 150.

16. Walker, 166.

17. Walker, 162.

sis of #CripTheVote's influence to the 2020 election and into the present moment, the extent of the influence, not just on disability studies but on politics in general, becomes even clearer.

From Campaign to Movement

Although published in 2020, Walker's analysis focused on the chats #CripTheVote organized prior to the 2016 election, not on how the campaign carried on and adapted after the 2016 election. In the wake of Trump's election, and the resulting policy decisions that had a directly negative impact on disabled people, the co-partners of #CripTheVote announced an "expanded vision thanks to the participation of the disability community."[18] Charting the future of #CripTheVote, the co-partners came up with a list of specific things #CripTheVote would do going forward, which included: "Remain online, community-based, and as decentralized as possible"; "Expand our focus beyond voting to other forms of political participation"; "Provide a space for conversation as a stimulus to collective action"; and "Partner with disabled people and organizations in broadening our movement's perspectives and expertise."[19] This expanded vision revealed what I see as a strength of the group: its ability to reflect on and adapt its approach based on input from and in collaboration with the many participants in its conversations. Or, put another way, #CripTheVote demonstrates democracy in action as a kind of online disabled chorus, to adapt an image of the chorus as multitude from Saidiya Hartman's *Wayward Lives, Beautiful Experiments,* in which she documents the "experiments with freedom" of young Black women in cities in the twentieth cen-

18. Gregg Beratan, Andrew Pulrang, and Alice Wong, "Looking Ahead: The Future of #CripTheVote," *Disability Visibility* blog, November 17, 2016, https://disabilityvisibilityproject.com/2016/11/17/looking-ahead-the-future -of-cripthevote/.

19. Beratan, Pulrang, and Wong, "Looking Ahead."

tury.[20] Hartman explores different spaces in the city—"the hallway, bedroom, stoop, rooftop, airshaft, and kitchenette [that] provided the space of experiment."[21] The online spaces created by hashtags that I am describing here are a different kind of—virtual—space for experimentation than what Hartman captures in her historical account of young Black women's practices of freedom in U.S. cities in the afterlife of slavery, but I want to draw a connection through the evocative image of the chorus, or what Hartman calls "the acts of collaboration and improvisation that unfold within the space of enclosure."[22] For disabled people, hashtags like #CripTheVote are portals to disability community and allow for collaboration and improvisation to unfold within the spaces of enclosure of stigma and ableism that prevent access to public spaces and reduce opportunities for participation in civic life.

Despite, or perhaps because of, Trump's election in 2016, #CripTheVote's online presence grew and its influence in building a cross-disability and intersectional crip community is hard to overstate. In 2017 alone, #CripTheVote hosted eleven chats, as well as three spotlight chats with disabled candidates in October 2017, including the one mentioned above with Carrie Ann Lucas. In a Year in Review blogpost, the three co-partners called 2017 an "interesting and tumultuous year" in which "we have seen the disability community under attack, defending against various legislation, policies, and actions by the current administration."[23] The Twitter chats covered a range of topics, including "Protecting the ADA and Disability Rights" in March, Trump's "First 100 Days" in April, "Media Coverage of Disabled People in the Age of Trump" in

---

20. Saidiya Hartman, *Wayward Lives, Beautiful Experiments: Intimate Histories of Riotous Black Girls, Troublesome Women, and Queer Radicals* (New York: Norton, 2019), xv.

21. Hartman, 61.

22. Hartman, 348.

23. Gregg Beratan, Andrew Pulrang, and Alice Wong, "2017: Year in Review," #CripTheVote blog, December 31, 2017, http://cripthevote .blogspot.com/2017/.

June, "Healthcare Activism and Next Steps" in October, and "Mental Health, Ableism and Elected Officials" in December, to name the focus of just some of the chats held during the busy year. Rather than folding up shop after the 2016 election, #CripTheVote intensified and expanded its campaign. Increasing the political participation of disabled people was still the campaign's primary objective, but what participation is, conceptually and in action, became a more prominent part of the conversation. Just as disability is a multiplicity, how one does disability and illness politics is also a multiplicity, and this is clear from the way #CripTheVote's online tactics and strategies complemented ADAPT's direct-action politics in 2017.

#CripTheVote in 2020

#CripTheVote's influential Twitter chats continued throughout Trump's presidency. In the run-up to the 2020 presidential election, #CripTheVote brought disability and illness politics to the general public's attention through high-profile Twitter chats with presidential candidates Elizabeth Warren and Pete Buttigieg. And as the United States and other nations went into lockdown because of the Covid-19 global pandemic, #CripTheVote also highlighted the problem of racial health disparities and the experiences of high-risk and immunocompromised people in the pandemic.

On January 7, 2020, #CripTheVote held a Twitter Town Hall Presidential Candidate Chat with Senator Elizabeth Warren.[24] In introducing the candidate chat, Wong, using the @DisVisibility Twitter account, welcomed everyone, and linked to Senator

24. As Wong (@SFdirewolf) noted in response to a reply to a tweet from her announcing #CripTheVote's "first ever candidate chat," this was not the first presidential candidate to have a forum with a disabled audience. As Wong explained, "@JulianCastro held a Twitter town hall with @IntersectedCrip [Sandy Ho, founder and coorganizer of the Disability and Intersectionality Summit] recently" and she linked to a wakelet from that event. Alice Wong, January 5, 2020, 9:00 pm, https://twitter.com/SFdirewolf/status/1214003738714619904.

Warren's plan for "Protecting the Rights and Equality of People with Disabilities."[25] Senator Warren's plan begins with a brief history of disability activism and several images of disabled activists:

> From bus blockades in Denver, Section 504 sit-ins in San Francisco, and the Deaf President Now student movement in D.C. to protests outside of Mitch McConnell's office and virtual marches, disability activists across the country have organized over decades to bring the nation's attention to the injustices they face. Fighting a world that has excluded, exploited, and institutionalized them, they have put their lives on the line for a more just future and changed this country for the better for everyone.[26]

In the second paragraph, Warren's plan mentions by name several disabled activists—Judith Heumann, Joyce Ardell Jackson, Justin Dart, Ed Roberts, Lois Curtis, and Anita Cameron are all named—but also emphasizes the "thousands of others" who have "won hard-fought civil rights victories that reshaped the way our country treats individuals with disabilities."[27] The plan then notes that 2020 is the thirtieth anniversary of the Americans with Disabilities Act and the one-hundredth anniversary of the Vocational Rehabilitation Program and argues that much progress has been made but that "we still have a lot of ground left to cover."[28] Warren asserts that, "As President, I will work in partnership with the disability community to combat ableism," before listing the plan's four main goals: "equal opportunity, full participation, independent living, and economic self sufficiency."[29] This is just the preamble for what is an incredibly

25. Alice Wong, January 7, 2020, 1:30 pm, https://twitter.com /DisVisibility/status/1214615182363840512. Senator Warren's plan, "Protecting the Rights and Equality of People with Disabilities," is still available on her website: https://elizabethwarren.com/plans/disability -rights-and-equality/.

26. "Protecting the Rights and Equality of People with Disabilities." Hyperlinks take readers to news articles about each of the protests mentioned in this opening paragraph.

27. "Protecting the Rights and Equality of People with Disabilities."

28. "Protecting the Rights and Equality of People with Disabilities."

29. "Protecting the Rights and Equality of People with Disabilities."

detailed and comprehensive plan that recognizes both the problem of systemic ableism and the potential for and importance of the participation of disabled people in public life and civil society.

In a tweet just before the #CripTheVote chat, Warren posted a short video where she said she was looking forward to "our first ever Twitter Town Hall."[30] As I noted in a quote retweet in response, it seemed appropriate (and momentous!) that Warren's first ever Twitter town hall was on "the topic of disability rights and justice because disabled activists have used social media very effectively to organize." And, I also argued, "#CripTheVote is one of the best examples of this activism in action."[31] The chat generated an enthusiastic response from disabled people on Twitter, as well as some coverage in the mainstream press. For example, Zack Budryk covered the chat for *The Hill*, noting that Warren confirmed in the chat that her campaign included disabled staffers, tweeting, "We have staff with disabilities across the campaign. Their lived experiences and talents help foster an inclusive and accessible campaign."[32] Budryk interviewed Gregg Beratan after the event, who said, "We are thrilled with how it went." He added that the organizers got what they had hoped for: "genuine engagement from the candidate." He also emphasized that the chat was a success not simply because Warren and her team took the time to answer #CripTheVote's questions that they supplied to her in advance, but that she "got to see so many of the questions from the community even if she couldn't answer them all. Over the five years that we have been doing this, the people participating have consistently pointed out that all policy issues are disability policy issues. [. . .] To hear that come back

---

30. Elizabeth Warren, January 7, 2020, 1:27 pm, https://twitter.com/ewarren/status/1214614548830965760.

31. Lisa Diedrich, January 7, 2020, 1:31 pm, https://twitter.com/lldiedrich/status/1214615563189866498.

32. Zack Budryk, "Warren Holds Twitter Town Hall with Disabled Activists," *The Hill*, January 7, 2020, https://thehill.com/homenews/campaign/477221-warren-participates-in-twitter-town-hall-with-disabled-activists/.

to us from a major candidate was fantastic."[33] The chat trended on Twitter, signaling to other political candidates and the public that disability was a topic of considerable importance, but also that it acted as a lens through which to view and analyze other topics—health care, education, housing, labor, immigration, and so on. In this way, electoral politics was "cripped" through a Twitter chat using the hashtag #CripTheVote.[34]

#CripTheVote on Pandemic Precarities

The online community created by the #CripTheVote hashtag and Twitter chats became even more important with the arrival of the coronavirus pandemic and lockdowns in spring 2020. On May 17, 2020, #CripTheVote held a Twitter chat on the coronavirus and health disparities with guest hosts Anita Cameron (@ADAPTanita) and Dustin Gibson (@notthreefifths), which would be the first of three chats, thus far, dealing with the impact of Covid-19 on disabled and immunocompromised people.[35] Wong, tweeting from her @DisVisibility account, promoted the chat and, along with

33. Budryk.
34. As happens relatively frequently during #CripTheVote chats, especially ones that trend as the chat with Senator Warren did, some Twitter users think the "crip" in #CripTheVote refers to the street gang in Los Angeles and express surprise in discovering this other use in the hashtag. There have also been some concerns about the use of "crip" because of its history as a derogatory term for disabled people. In a post on the #CripTheVote website, Andrew Pulrang offers some "Notes on 'Crip'" to explain the reasons the co-partners opted to use "crip" in the hashtag. He begins by noting that "Selective use of 'crip' or 'crippled' by people with disabilities is a conscious act of empowerment through 'reclaiming' a former slur as a badge of pride." He also argues the term can be "used ironically, to convey a bit of edginess, humor, and confidence, from a community that people tend to assume will be sad, bitter, and boring," Pulrang, "#CripTheVote: Notes On 'Crip,'" Disability Thinking blog, March 29, 2016, https://disabilitythinking.com /disabilitythinking/2016/3/28/cripthevote-notes-on-crip.
35. Along with the chat in May 2020, #CripTheVote has also held Twitter chats on "Coronavirus and the 2020 Elections" on September 27, 2020, and on "Pandemic Policy" on January 16, 2022.

the #CripTheVote hashtag, added several other hashtags for the topic, including: #HighRiskCovid19, #NoBodyIsDisposable, and #WeAreEssential.[36] As is always the case with #CripTheVote Twitter chats, this chat was incredibly well-organized with a list of eight questions prepared and distributed in advance that covered both general, overarching topics (e.g., "Q3 How does systemic racism, ableism, and other forms of oppression result in health disparities and disproportionate impact on Black, brown, and indigenous communities?") and more specific situations, for example for institutionalized persons (e.g. "Q6: Sites of confinement, like nursing facilities, prisons/jails, 'detention' centers, institutions, group 'homes' and other congregate settings are experiencing rapid #COVID19 outbreaks and deaths. What kind of actions are needed to save lives?")[37] It is also important to note that the chat not only took up topics related to the experiences of disabled and high-risk people during the pandemic but also that the chat itself became a site for the practice of care and the enactment of survivance. The first question makes this disability-justice care work clear, asking, "How are YOU doing so far? How are you dealing with the challenges of staying at home or going out, getting your needs met, and keeping safe especially if you are high risk and/or immunocompromised?"[38]

Thus, the chat opens with a check-in and gives everyone tuning in for the chat (not just the organizers and the guest hosts) an opportunity to connect with others and express their fears, frustrations, and hopes. I have tuned in for many #CripTheVote chats and one of the most notable aspects of the conversations, in general, is how welcoming and encouraging the coorganizers are to everyone who

36. Alice Wong, May 15, 2020, 2 p.m., https://mobile.twitter.com /DisVisibility/status/1261355670168907776.
37. "May 17, 2020 #CripTheVote Twitter Chat: Coronavirus and Health Disparities," May 11, 2020. http://cripthevote.blogspot.com/2020/05 /may-17-2020-cripthevote-twitter-chat.html.
38. "May 17, 2020 #CripTheVote Twitter Chat: Coronavirus and Health Disparities." Emphasis in original.

joins. Especially in the pandemic, this care work is key to providing community and crip solidarity for high-risk and immunocompromised people who have been increasingly isolated by the threat of the coronavirus and have, understandably, felt "demoralized" by repeated policy failures, as Andrew Pulrang put it in his tweet introducing himself in the coronavirus and health disparities chat.[39] Other participants expressed exhaustion from the effort to keep safe, trauma from witnessing mass sickness and death, and despair at the shocking disregard for the lives of disabled people, people of color (who make up the majority of "essential" workers), and incarcerated and other institutionalized people. And, even at this relatively early stage of the pandemic, there was already a critique of what Dustin Gibson identified as "attempts to return back to 'normalcy.'"[40] While the chats are scheduled at a particular time and usually last an hour (or sometimes only a half an hour), the coorganizers always emphasize that the hashtag allows a person to check out, and even participate in, the chat later and at their own pace. The resources provided by the chat are there to be discovered later, but so too, potentially, is the online disability community that the hashtag enacts.[41]

The Future of Disability Twitter

I end this chapter with this important point about the multiple temporalities for enacting online disability community afforded

39. Andrew Pulrang, May 17, 2020, 7:03 p.m., @AndrewPulrang.
40. Dustin Gibson, May 17, 2020, 7:10 p.m., @notthreefifths.
41. In *Crip Kinship*, Kafai interviews community organizer and culture worker Lilac Vylette Maldonado, who identifies as "a sick, disabled, neuro-divergent, two-spirit Chicanx femme," about "finding crip kinship online." Maldonado beautifully describes the potentiality of such a space: "Over the frayed threads of the web, a framework for survival has been lovingly yet imperfectly created by those of us who are brave enough to imagine a kinder, better, freer world than the one we inherited. This is the framework of our kinship, it is our breadcrumb trail to liberation," 119. Hashtags like #CripTheVote also function as a breadcrumb trail to liberation.

by the #CripTheVote hashtag and chats because, as I write, the future of Twitter, recently purchased by Elon Musk, remains in the balance. As many have noted on and off Twitter since Musk's acquisition, although far from perfect, Twitter has been a lifeline for many disabled people. One early sign of Musk's, at best, lack of concern and, at worst, contempt for disabled Twitter users, is the firing of the entire Accessibility Experience Team, announced in a tweet by Gerard K. Cohen on November 4, 2022.[42] Cohen's tweet noted, "There aren't many people that have had the opportunity to make such an important global platform like Twitter accessible, but we understood the mission."[43] In one accessibility feature created just before the firing of the Accessibility Experience Team, Twitter added an image description reminder as an opt-in feature for users. As Mia Sato noted in an article in *The Verge* about the new feature, "The introduction of alt text reminders is a long time coming— disability activists and allies have lobbied Twitter for more tools around alt text and have asked sighted users to be more consistent with adding alt text to images."[44]

Rather than end with Musk's ableism and the potential loss of Twitter as a space for creating the conditions of possibility for disabled participation in U.S. politics and culture, I end this chapter with an image and image description of #CripTheVote created by artist Micah Bazant and available on the #CripTheVote blog (Figure 4). On their website, Bazant describes themselves as a "visual artist and cultural strategist who works with social justice movements to reimagine the world. They create art inspired by struggles to end white supremacy, patriarchy, ableism, and transphobia."[45] One of Bazant's best-known images is a gorgeous poster

42. Gerard K. Cohen, November 4, 2022, 1:30 p.m., @geraldkcohen.

43. Gerard K. Cohen, November 4, 2022, 1:30 p.m., @geraldkcohen.

44. Mia Sato, "Twitter's Latest Feature Is a Tool to Make Your Feed More Accessible," *The Verge*, September 19, 2022, https://www.theverge.com/2022/9/19/23357145/twitters-alt-text-reminders-expansion-image-descriptions-accessibility.

45. https://www.micahbazant.com/about.

Figure 4. #CripTheVote graphic by artist Micah Bazant. Image description: Illustration with large red text: "Crip the Vote" above two disabled queer people of color surrounded by flowers and radiating love. One person is Black, uses a wheelchair and a ventilator, and has a drink with a plastic straw on her tray. A butterfly is resting on her wrist. The other person is Chinese American, fat and uses a cane." http://cripthevote.blogspot.com/2020/10/cripthevote-graphic-by-artist-micah .html. Reprinted with permission of Micah Bazant and Alice Wong.

of trans activist Marsha P. Johnson with the phrase "No Pride for Some of Us Without Liberation for All of Us," which was created for LGBTQ+ Pride celebrations in 2013 and has since circulated widely as an inspiration for trans and queer racial justice work. Bazant's "Crip the Vote" image, produced in October 2020 in collaboration with Alice Wong and *Disability Visibility* to showcase the work of #CripTheVote, is a similarly joyful image of politics in action. On their Instagram page, Bazant frames the image in relation to voting rights for disabled people, adding a long caption about accessible and inaccessible voting that begins: "Access is love. We all have the right to voting access! If you need support you have the right to have a person of your choice help you register, research and cast your vote without pressure or unwanted influence."[46] Thus, the image of two disabled people of color leaning into each other makes visible how access is love. It also makes visible what #CripTheVote has made possible: disability community, solidarity, and love.

46. Micah Bazant, October 23, 2020, micahbazant, https://www .instagram.com/p/CGsxqPbgpmx/. The phrase "access is love" refers to the hashtag #AccessIsLove created by Wong and Mia Mingus.

5. #TimeForUnrest

IN THIS CHAPTER, I take up the multiple temporalities of a specific chronic disabling condition—myalgic encephalomyelitis (ME) or chronic fatigue syndrome (CFS)—through an analysis of ME/CFS experiences and events as documented in Jennifer Brea's film *Unrest* (2017)[1] and on social media via ME/CFS-related hashtags. Brea's film shows illness and illness politics as operating biopychosocially across different spaces and temporalities, including on social media, which becomes a site of a kind of embodied assembly where people gather while remaining at home and in their own beds. In her book on precarity and public assembly, *Notes Toward a Performative Theory of Assembly,* Judith Butler explores the "question of whether the destitute are outside of politics and power or are in fact living out a political agency and resistance that expose the policing of boundaries of the sphere of appearance itself."[2] I also explore this question of how those deemed outside the limits of the political—in this case the sick and bedbound—nonetheless, as Butler posits, "break into the sphere of appearance as from the outside, as its outside, confounding the distinction between inside and outside."[3] Brea's film and related hashtags on social media

---

1. Jennifer Brea, dir., *Unrest*. August 24, 2017. Video; 98 mins. Shella Films and Little by Little Films. https://vimeo.com/ondemand/unrest.

2. Butler, *Notes Toward a Performative Theory of Assembly,* 78.

3. Butler, 78.

create the conditions of possibility of this breakthrough into the sphere of appearance, despite how, or perhaps because, such action exhausts—literally, in the case of ME/CFS—any one individual's capacity to appear.

Brea's film presents what I call the historical persistence of hysteria, a diagnostic category replaced by conversion disorder, but nonetheless haunting the phenomenological experience of illnesses, like ME/CFS, without (yet) known biological causes. At the same time, the film also attempts to capture the experience of embodiment as a kind of endurance, as extreme fatigue and sensitivity to light, sound, and surroundings makes ME/CFS a condition of unrest—a disturbed and uneasy state that is at once physical, social, and political. Early in the film, as Brea films herself with her phone struggling to crawl across the floor to her bed, she anticipates a question that might be on the viewer's mind: "Why would I film it?" Her answers—"Because I think someone should see this" and "I didn't know what else to do so I just kept filming"—suggest both a politics of visibility and a politics of endurance, or the politics of making endurance visible through practices of documenting illness and illness politics that connects to other historical and contemporary examples of illness and disability in action, including, importantly, to the emergent illness of long Covid in the present, which I will touch on in this chapter and discuss in more detail in my conclusion.

As with #CripTheVote, Brea, her film, and the hashtags #TimeForUnrest and #MillionsMissing, among others, challenge in important ways what activism and the figure of the activist look like. By connecting with people with ME/CFS online, Brea not only documents their experiences with ME/CFS but also seeks to politicize the lack of participation of people with ME/CFS whom she describes as missing in action from society and the public sphere. With the film and hashtags, Brea demonstrates illness (in)action as a kind of unrest cure. I conclude this chapter by discussing the recent protest in September 2022 organized by the #MEAction Network that took place in front of the White House and on social media to draw attention to the continued underfunding of research on ME/CFS, despite increased interest in understanding the long-term impact of viral infections with the emergence and widespread experiences of long Covid. My goal in highlighting this recent demonstration of illness politics is itself meant as a form of illness politics, as is this book itself—that is, as participating in, by amplifying and extending, a "struggle for an egalitarian social and political order in which a livable interdependency becomes possible," as Butler calls for in her lecture on "Bodies in Alliance and the Politics of the Street."[4]

Hysteria as Ur-Illness Performative

Brea presents her own experience of illness as personally, phenomenologically, and politically confounding. Clips from home movies show an active little girl and more recent film footage and still photographs give a glimpse of an adventurous young woman always on the move and determined, as she puts it, to "swallow the world whole." This visibly active life ends when Brea is twenty-eight. While working on her doctorate at Harvard, she gets sick with a very high fever and ends up bedridden. She is exhausted in a way she has never felt before, the side of her face becomes numb, sometimes she is unable to speak or think coherently, and she becomes sensitive to light and sounds. She sees "every kind of specialist," but no one can say exactly what is wrong. Eventually, a neurologist diagnoses "conversion disorder," speculating that the likely cause is either a distant trauma that she doesn't fully remember or recent stress from preparing for doctoral exams. "Conversion disorder" is a new term for an old illness: hysteria. The term itself emerged in 1980 as part of the bio-scientizing, "evidence-based" impulse of the third edition of psychology's *Diagnostic and Statistical Manual* (*DSM-III*) and is defined as a "psychoneurosis in which bodily symptoms (such as paralysis of the limbs) appear without physical basis."[5] With its

---

4. Butler, 69.
5. Merriam-Webster online dictionary, https://www.merriam-webster.com/medical/somatoform%20disorder.

ever-changing terminology and multitude of somatoforms, hysteria operates historically like the diagnosis itself: the category appears to suffer from conversion disorder, or put another way, we might say, diagnostically, hysteria is hysterical.

A short history of hysteria is at the center of Brea's film, which presents the experience and event of hysteria as a slide show. A series of black-and-white, historical images of hysterics flash by, accompanied by a syncopated beat, the combination of image and sonic reverberation heightening the feeling of the persistence of hysteria as a repetition compulsion of a diagnostic category that is characterized by a certain photogenicity. *Unrest*'s historical hysterics are all women and Brea's treatment of them suggests the importance of the still and moving photographic image in enacting hysteria across different times and spaces.

Hysteria has a long association with the female body and women. The symptoms and significations that concatenate around the sign of hysteria are multiple and mobile. Hysteria's habit of mimicking other diseases makes hysteria not one disease but many if not all diseases, at least potentially. As I argued in chapter 3, illness and illness politics are performative, understood in the way Butler uses the term in relation to her theories of gender and precarity.[6] These theories have been utilized to discern, importantly, the how not the what of gender, and I argue that they help us to analyze the how not the what of gender (along with race, class, sexuality) and illness together.[7] Where illness is concerned, the utterance

6. See, for example, my piece "Illness as Assemblage: The Case of Hystero-epilepsy," *Body & Society* 21, no. 3 (September 2015): 66–90.

7. In her lecture on "Gender Politics and the Right to Appear" in *Notes Toward a Performative Theory of Assembly,* Butler explores a question she is often asked about the links between her analysis of the performativity of gender with her later analysis of precarity. She reckons "it is possible to see how precarity has always been in this picture, since gender performativity was a theory and practice, one might say, that opposed the unlivable conditions in which gender and sexual minorities live (and sometimes also those gender majorities who 'passed' as normative at very high psychic and somatic costs)," 33.

"you have ____ [choose any disease here]" doesn't simply name an existing biological condition; it brings that condition into being. When certain conditions and procedures are met—the authority of a doctor making the diagnosis, conclusive lab work and test results—then a person can be said to be ill. When these conditions are not met, then the person often becomes mentally rather than physically ill.[8]

Hysteria as conversion disorder becomes a kind of ur-illness performative, as the default category that has persisted over time for illnesses not yet explained biologically. This repeated "not yet" helps explain, I think, hysteria's persistent yet divergent and multiple enactments. *Unrest*'s syncopated slide show of hysteria visually captures hysteria as ur-illness performative. Although Brea refuses the diagnosis of conversion disorder for herself, she nonetheless links her experience to the history of hysteria and its visual somatoforms. Her desire to document her own and others' experiences of ME/CFS is motivated by an understanding that the past isn't so "strange and distant"—people, women mostly, are still being locked up in institutions or trapped in bedrooms they never leave because their illnesses are not treated as real. Brea believes we should know and do better now, but she comes to realize from her own experience of illness and from documenting illness—hers and others', past and present—that "we're still doing this," still doing hysteria. This is what Ed Yong, reporting on Covid "long haulers," calls the "long history of medical gaslighting," in which a patient's physical suffering is downplayed "as being all in their head, or caused by stress or

8. Sara Ahmed's concept of the nonperformative is useful here. Ahmed discusses this in the context of institutional diversity "commitments" that don't change the institution in any meaningful way, *On Being Included: Racism and Diversity in Institutional Life* (Durham, N.C.: Duke University Press, 2012). I would argue that diagnostic nonperformatives work to contain illnesses of unknown etiologies so that they are not a problem for medicine and its cognitive and social authority.

anxiety."[9] I will return to the experience and event of long Covid in my conclusion to this chapter, as well as in the final chapter, and to work by activists and some scientists to make connections between the symptomatology of long Covid and ME/CFS as a form of illness politics that seeks to counteract medical gaslighting.

Finding a Phenomenological Vocabulary of Illness

Bedridden for several years and living in limbo without a conclusive diagnosis, Brea describes how her once wide world shrinks to one room. She begins to search online for possible clues to what has caused and what might treat her intractable condition. Her own research leads her to what she will discover is the still somewhat controversial diagnosis of ME/CFS and to a whole community of sufferers in the shadows of society. As Brea writes in her director's statement, she "fell down this rabbit hole and discovered a hidden world of thousands of patients all around the globe, many of whom are homebound or confined to their beds and use the internet to connect with each other and the outside world."[10] Along with documenting her own experience of ME/CFS, Brea is determined to document the lives of others—some 17 million worldwide, the #MillionsMissing, as proclaimed by another hashtag generated by the film to highlight the problem of lack of visibility and research on the problem of ME/CFS.

The lack of visibility and research on ME/CFS is a result of the fact that doctors and scientists can't find a biological cause and so doubt the realness of the illness except as a present-day form of hysteria, hence the conversion disorder diagnosis. In her book

9. Ed Yong, "COVID-19 Can Last for Several Months," *The Atlantic*, June 4, 2020, https://www.theatlantic.com/health/archive/2020/06/covid-19-coronavirus-longterm-symptoms-months/612679/.

10. Jennifer Brea, "Director's Statement," https://static1.squarespace.com/static/597750f4d2b857b95a7e537e/t/59c2b618e3df28b1658595b8/1505932827580/UNREST_Press_Kit_August.pdf.

The Rejected Body, feminist philosopher Susan Wendell discusses how chronic illnesses and illnesses with unknown etiologies are a problem for medicine. Medicine tends to dismiss or deny the existence of what it cannot explain physiologically or treat successfully. Medicine has significant cognitive and social authority in contemporary society, affecting, Wendell argues, "how we experience our bodies and our selves, how our society describes our experiences and validates/invalidates them, how our society supports or fails to support our bodily sufferings and struggles, and what our culture knows about the human body."[11] Wendell's interest in the philosophical importance of chronic illness and disability emerges out of her own experience with ME, which, as with Brea, came on suddenly and devastatingly in February 1985. Unlike Brea, Wendell is "very lucky" in relation to her doctors, who "recognized at once that something was seriously wrong,"[12] and found evidence in blood tests that indicated a viral infection. She saw specialists in infectious disease and immunology and was first diagnosed with acute infectious mononucleosis, then chronic Epstein-Barr virus syndrome, before doctors finally arrived at the then newly emergent diagnosis ME. Wendell notes that the "history of my own illness has coincided with the gradual discovery of ME/CFIDS [chronic fatigue immune dysfunction syndrome] by the rest of the world."[13] She describes learning to live with chronic pain, muscle weakness, "profound fatigue (much more total and exhausting than any fatigue [she] experienced when healthy)," dizziness, depression, headaches, problems recalling words, etc.[14]

Wendell provides an especially astute critique of what she calls the able-bodied paradigm of humanity, which relies on an idealized view of the body as young, healthy, and always up to speed. Twenty

---

11. Susan Wendell, *The Rejected Body: Feminist Philosophical Reflections on Disability* (New York: Routledge, 1996), 119.

12. Wendell, 2.

13. Wendell, 2.

14. Wendell, 3.

years after the publication of Wendell's incisive critique, Brea's film documents the still significant difficulties people with ME/CFS have in finding validation for their phenomenological experiences of their bodies. Wendell offers insight here as well. She tells a story about how she came to realize she had to be cautious in how she described her symptoms when a specialist showed surprise when she used the vivid metaphor of being injected with strong poison to capture how she felt at the moments her illness relapsed. Very early in *Unrest*, as Brea and her husband Omar Wasow wait to see a doctor, they discuss a similar discursive tightrope: "if you say too little, they can't help you," Omar says. "If you say too much, they think you're a mental patient." Wendell argues that what medicine lacks is an effective vocabulary for the phenomenology of illness. She explains that patient-support groups are valuable in that they "offer a context in which people who are ill can work together to articulate their experiences of their bodies, to find or invent a phenomenological vocabulary that is adequate." This is what Brea's film and illness politics in general also does: find or invent a phenomenological vocabulary for illness, updating and extending Wendell's support group by connecting to others online. And, as we are seeing in the present, the phenomenological vocabulary and online illness politics of ME/CFS provides a portal into the confounding experiences of long Covid, which shares many symptoms, including debilitating fatigue, with ME/CFS.

Brea's description of her phenomenological experience of ME/CFS is remarkably like Wendell's. Both discuss a "cellular exhaustion," as Wendell puts it, or becoming less and less effective at the cellular level, as Brea says. Wendell anticipates the dismissive reactions to such a theory of cellular experience: "Certainly I do not experience my body as cellular, but I experience the exhaustion as so deep and pervasive that it feels as though something is wrong throughout my body on the cellular level."[15] Brea moves between scales, from questions about the metabolic crash point and how

15. Wendell, 135.

that feels—"when we crash we disappear"—to questions that after thirty years still need to be asked: "Why do more women get it? Is it genetic? Why thirty years later are we no closer to a cure?" For Brea, it is #TimeForUnrest, and her film and advocacy work operate across multiple temporalities and spaces to bring illness (in)action into the public.

The narrative arc of Brea's film is from rest to unrest, from passivity to activity, and from private to public. Brea explains that what terrifies her is that "you can disappear because someone is telling the wrong story about you." Thus, *Unrest* seeks to tell a truer story, but also to make visible the "millions missing" from public life. The film doesn't end with triumph but with images of protest and a statement of endurance and repetition: "I am still here. I am still here."

"Still Sick, Still Fighting"

As with my discussions of #ADAPTandRESIST and #CripTheVote, I want to end this chapter by showing how the struggle that Brea documents in her film continues in the present—or, as in a recent slogan created by ME/CFS activists, "still sick, still fighting." Again, this is one of the key functions of hashtags: to expand and extend the parameters of an action beyond a particular space and time—into the present and the future. In September 2022, the #MEAction Network, which describes itself on its website as "igniting a global revolution in ME care," organized a #MillionsMissing protest in front of the White House in Washington, D.C., and online. The goal of this protest was to "tell President Biden that the pandemic is not over, and that millions are being disabled with post-viral disease, including Long COVID and ME/CFS."[16] The protest was a demonstration of both illness and illness politics that I would argue, following Butler, brought "the material urgencies of the body into the square"

16. "Protest at the White House to Tell President Biden 'Pandemic Is NOT Over," September 19, 2022, https://www.meaction.net/2022/09/19 /protest-at-white-house-to-tell-president-biden-pandemic-is-not-over/.

and made "those needs central to the demands of politics."[17] In her series of lectures on the performativity of assembly, Butler is interested in moments "when precarious lives assemble on the street in forms of alliance that must struggle to achieve the space of appearance."[18] In the case of the #MillionsMissing protest, one form of alliance that was demonstrated was between people sick with ME/CFS and people sick with long Covid. As Ben HsuBorger, a person with ME/CFS and #MEAction advocacy director, explained about the protesters: "We are sick and disabled with ME/CFS and Long COVID but are here today, putting our bodies on the line" to send a clear message that "we need urgent action from our government."[19]

#MEAction Network documented the protest with a livestream on Twitter that was watched by more than nine thousand viewers that day, and clips of which have since been uploaded to YouTube (Figure 5). Coverage on the #MEAction website emphasized the material urgencies of these bodies in public and an #MEAction press release documented the impact of the protest on the protesters' bodies: "The protesters—most of them sick with ME/CFS and/or Long COVID—struggled to go on as their symptoms worsened with the exertion of chanting, walking and being in the heat. They will now spend days 'crashed' in bed with worsened symptoms attempting to recover from the hours they spent making their voices heard."[20] Other press coverage also highlighted the protest as a demonstration of illness in action. Zeynep Tufekci, opinion columnist and author of *Twitter and Tear Gas,* wrote about the protest for the *New York Times* in late October 2022 in a piece entitled "Protesters So Ill, They Couldn't Get Arrested."[21]

17. Butler, *Notes Toward a Performative Theory of Assembly,* 96.
18. Butler, 86.
19. "Protest at the White House to Tell President Biden 'Pandemic Is NOT Over.'"
20. "Protest at the White House to Tell President Biden 'Pandemic Is NOT Over.'"
21. Zeynep Tufekci, "Protesters So Ill, They Couldn't Get Arrested," *New York Times,* October 29, 2022, A-22, https://www.nytimes.com/2022/10/27/opinion/me-cfs-long-covid.html.

Figure 5. Screen grab from video of the #MEAction Network protest at the White House on September 19, 2022. Protesters are lying on the sidewalk in front of the fence around the White House and holding up signs that say, for example, "URGENT ACTION NEEDED" and "STILL SICK, STILL FIGHTING." Closed captioning says, "We've increased attention to ME through the media, lobbied. . . . ," https:// youtu.be/qnnb2CL0VKY.

Tufekci's piece begins with a story about one of the protesters, Gabriel San Emeterio, who is HIV positive and has ME/CFS and who tells Tufekci that HIV "has been less onerous" than ME/CFS, which Tufekci calls "this more obscure affliction."[22] Tufekci then describes the protesters as giving "their best shot at civil disobedience" but adds that "instead of being arrested, they were largely ignored."[23] This narrative of a failed protest relies on the image of the heroic activist in the streets defying the police and the law to risk arrest and generate media attention for their cause. The aftermath for this #MillionsMissing protest in front of the White House was not disruption, arrest, and imprisonment. Rather, as Tufekci reports, the aftermath was the appearance of a symptom of the protesters' conditions—post-exertional malaise (PEM), which is experienced by people with both ME/CFS and long Covid. Tufekci discusses

22. Tufekci, A-22.
23. Tufekci, A-22.

how "PEM may be one reason ME/CFS, and even long Covid, has been dismissed so often as a serious condition by many doctors."[24] Tufekci discusses how a symptom like post-exertional malaise is stigmatized as a sign of an unwillingness to push through illness. She notes that this glorification of pushing through is part of an ableist culture of medicine, in which medical training normalizes pushing through exhaustion as part of the process of becoming a doctor. Thus, an antagonism can arise between doctors and those patients deemed not sick but malingering.

However, Tufekci's coverage of the protest and its aftermath is key: as with the ADAPT activists on Capitol Hill, the protest becomes a spectacle of illness politics when the media covers it as such. Tufekci asks a question that has been central to my analysis of illness politics on social media: "How do you protest when the very act is a dire threat to what little ability you have left?"[25] Yet, she makes the mistake of assuming that the only playbook to follow is the one "AIDS activists used years ago, escalating civil disobedience."[26] She then describes a cat-and-mouse game with police on the day of the protest, in which the police managed to direct traffic around protesters lying in the street and, in the end, the protesters' failure to escalate as they became exhausted from their efforts to appear in public. Yet, I contend that, in the case of the #MillionsMissing protest, the spectacle is not civil disobedience and arrest but a less visible, yet no less powerful, form of embodied resistance—the willingness to make oneself sicker to draw attention to one's illness and the politics surrounding it. In her analysis of hunger strikes in prisons, Butler argues that "bodily exposure can take different forms."[27] Her point that "sometimes deliberately exposing the body to possible harm is part of the very meaning of political resistance" is relevant in the case of the #MillionsMissing

24. Tufekci, A-22.
25. Tufekci, A-22.
26. Tufekci, A-22.
27. Butler, *Notes Toward a Performative Theory of Assembly*, 125.

protest. The activists who participated in the protests at the White House and online demonstrated "what it means to mobilize vulnerability in concert."[28] In concert is not simply on the street but beyond it through the hashtag on social media that continues the mobilizing of vulnerability in concert, even as the activists return home and to their beds to recover from the exertion of their illness politics.

28. Butler, 140.

Ongoingness: #LongCOVID

MY CONCLUSION doesn't so much end the conversation as point to ongoing conversations about illness and illness politics through the lens of the emergent condition long Covid. I began this book by looking at #IllnessPolitics as an ableist form of electoral politics, focusing on campaigns and hashtags to discredit Hillary Clinton and Donald Trump in the 2016 and 2020 U.S. presidential elections. I then shifted focus from hashtags directed at individuals running for office to several recent enactments of illness and disability politics organized by and for disabled and chronically ill people to counteract ableism and stigma and to build community and increase disabled and sick peoples' participation in public life. Through this trajectory—from stigmatizing and individualistic to destigmatizing and justice-oriented forms of illness politics—I have sought to demonstrate how fundamental illness politics is to contrasting visions of society. As I have argued in both the content and form of this project, it matters whether we see illness as disqualifying from public life or as a challenge and opportunity to make society more inclusive, accessible, and just.

I now move from a chapter on the phenomenological vocabulary and in-person and online illness politics of people with ME/CFS to what can only be an inconclusive concluding chapter on the condition long Covid, which shares many symptoms with ME/CFS, including debilitating fatigue and brain fog. I end with long Covid not as culmination of an argument about illness politics but as a reminder of the multiple spaces and temporalities of illness and as gesture to the ongoingness of illness politics on social media. The hashtag #LongCOVID was first used on social media on May 20, 2020, by Elisa Perego, an Honorary Research Associate at University College London who is from Lombardy, one of the first areas hard hit by Covid-19. Perego coined the term long Covid "as a contraction of long-term Covid illness, to summarize her experience of disease as cyclical, progressive, and multiphasic."[1] In June 2020, Ed Yong, one of the most important U.S.-based real-time chroniclers of the Covid-19 pandemic, published a piece in *The Atlantic,* "COVID-19 Can Last for Several Months," which would become just a first in-stantiation of the ongoing work by Yong and others of documenting the experience of Covid "long-haulers," some of whom, at that time, were in month three of a confounding illness experience character-ized by a wide variety of symptoms.[2] Yong centers patients' voices in his piece and introduces the long-haulers he interviews by noting how many days they have been sick, showing how they themselves are closely tracking their own illnesses, even as they find themselves "trapped in a statistical limbo, uncounted and thus overlooked."[3]

Long Covid as a condition with a complex symptomatology is still not well understood,[4] and although we are now more than

1. Felicity Callard and Elisa Perego, "How and Why Patients Made Long Covid," *Social Science and Medicine* 268 (2021), https://doi.org/10.1016 /j.socscimed.2020.113426.

2. Yong, "COVID-19 Can Last for Several Months."

3. Yong, n.p.

4. In an opinion piece for *The BMJ* published on October 1, 2020, Felicity Callard, Elisa Perego, and four others, offer five reasons for "Why We Need to Keep Using the Patient Made Term 'Long Covid'" (blogs.bmj. com, October 1, 2020, https://blogs.bmj.com/bmj/2020/10/01/why-we -need-to-keep-using-the-patient-made-term-long-covid/). In point number 1, they note that "Long Covid acknowledges that the cause and disease course are as yet unknown." For them, the strength of the term "is in its non-specificity."

three years into the Covid-19 pandemic as a mass disabling event, many people suffering from this debilitating chronic condition, especially BIPOC people, have had their embodied experiences denied and dismissed by doctors and others. Yet, as I have sought to demonstrate in this project, illness and disability politics on social media have created the conditions of possibility for people with long Covid to come together to fight for support, both clinical and social, and against stigma and ableism. What we see in the case of long Covid, then, is illness politics as a recursive phenomenon. On the one hand, people with long Covid have benefited from the work of disabled and chronically ill activists who have challenged stigma and ableism, increased participation in civil society and politics, and created support groups and built community among sick and disabled people. On the other hand, because of the large number of people impacted by long Covid, they now help make visible, for example, the #MillionsMissing of people with ME/CFS and other post-viral conditions and expand awareness of illness and disability politics more generally. Put simply, long-haulers both benefit from and extend across time and space the illness politics that has come before. In this conclusion, I first provide a brief genealogy of the term "long Covid" and its social-media origins before discussing a short documentary film created by Lindsey Sitz for *The Washington Post,* posted on its website in February 2021, and featuring Cynthia Adinig, a thirty-five-year-old Black woman with long Covid, who documented her own experience as a long-hauler and the repeated failures of medicine to take her and her illness seriously, as well as her work to connect with other long-haulers online.[5] Adinig's story of illness is both singular and unfortunately common, especially for women of color in America.

5. Lindsey Sitz, "Why This Black Woman with 'Long Covid' Feels the Medical Community Has Failed Her," *The Washington Post,* February 2, 2021, https://www.washingtonpost.com/video/topics/coronavirus/why-this -black-woman-with-long-covid-feels-the-medical-community-has-failed -her/2021/02/02/68ce212c-f1ba-4983-8d07-d2fd5e8e4429_video.html.

By telling her story on social media and in and through Sitz's film, Adinig demonstrates illness politics in action as care of the self and connection to others.

Making Long Covid

In their article in *Social Science and Medicine*, Felicity Callard and Elisa Perego, both of whom identify as having long Covid, argue that "patients made long Covid."[6] They point to a long history of health activism and illness politics, including by mental health survivors, AIDS activists, people with chronic illnesses, and other patient advocates. They note as well that, despite this long history of patient activism, nonetheless "patient and lay contributions have often been ignored or underacknowledged by conventional actors, which has intensified patient suffering and societal inequalities."[7] Callard and Perego explicitly pinpoint social media as a key site for the making of long Covid by patient advocates. Indeed, they write, affirming my argument in this book about the importance of social media as a site for illness politics, "There are strong reasons to argue that Long Covid is the first illness to be made through patients finding one another on Twitter and other social media."[8] Callard and Perego provide an extensive genealogy of how the term "long Covid" emerged, noting that, as early as March 2020, people were describing a multiplicity of lingering symptoms, even in cases that were designated "mild" because the person was never hospitalized. In May 2020, as part of the online journal *Somatosphere*'s "Dispatches from the Pandemic" series, Callard had already taken on the diagnostically and phenomenologically imprecise category "mild" in relation to Covid-19.[9] In tweeting the essay to her fol-

6. Callard and Perego, "How and Why Patients Made Long Covid," 1.
7. Callard and Perego, 1.
8. Callard and Perego, 2.
9. Felicity Callard, "Very, Very Mild: Covid-19 Symptoms and Illness Classification," *Somatosphere*, May 8, 2020, http://somatosphere.net/2020/mild-covid.html/.

lowers, Callard noted, following the emerging activist protocol of counting the days since one first developed symptoms for Covid, that she was on "Day 52" and that she was only able to write such a reflection on the days when her "own 'mild' #Covid19 symptoms have been manageable."[10]

Citing science studies scholar Lorraine Daston's work, Callard and Perego track how "long Covid" solidified into a "scientific object," "even as its precise contours remain subject to debate."[11] They discuss how peer-reviewed scientific studies showing cardiological and neurological sequelae even in cases of "mild" Covid-19 began to circulate on social media with the hashtag #LongCOVID in July 2020. They wonder, writing in October 2020, whether long Covid will persist as a term or "break up into other classifications."[12] As I write over two years later, it is now clear that the term "long Covid" has persisted, in no small part thanks to the ever-growing number of patient advocates who, nonetheless, still find themselves up against dismissive and disbelieving doctors.[13] Callard and Perego also discuss how racism, sexism, and ableism contribute to the dismissiveness and denialism surrounding patients' experiences of

10. Felicity Callard, May 9, 2020, 6:37 a.m., @felicitycallard.

11. Callard and Perego, "How and Why Patients Made Long Covid," 3. Callard and Perego cite Lorraine Daston, *Biographies of Scientific Objects* (Chicago: University of Chicago Press, 2000).

12. Callard and Perego, "How and Why Patients Made Long Covid," 3.

13. A recent study by the CDC that looked at "death certificate literal text to identify and quantify COVID-19 deaths with post-acute sequelae of COVID-19 (PASC), or long COVID, in the National Vital Statistics System (NVSS)" attempted to account for the multiplicity of terms used to describe the phenomenon long Covid. The study searched for the following terms on death certificates: chronic Covid, long Covid, long haul Covid, long hauler Covid, post-acute sequelae of Covid-19, post- acute sequelae SARS-CoV-2 infection, PASC, post Covid, and post Covid syndrome. Farida B. Ahmad et al., "Identification of Deaths with Post-acute Sequelae of COVID-19 from Death Certificate Literal Text: United States, January 1, 2020–June 30, 2022," *NVSS Vital Statistics Rapid Release*, Report No. 25, December 2022, https://www.cdc.gov/nchs/data/vsrr/vsrr025.pdf.

long Covid. They acknowledge that "patients from marginalized/ minoritized communities, many of whom are central to making Long Covid, have been denied platforms, and have decided not to place themselves in the spotlight to discuss a disease that compounds discrimination."[14] This returns us to a key aspect of illness politics—that it intersects with, and sometimes stands in for, racial, sexual, and class politics.

Medical Gaslighting: Cynthia Adinig's Story

In his article in June 2020, Yong discusses long Covid in relation to a "long history of medical gaslighting."[15] He notes that this phenomenon is gendered and that women are "less likely to be perceived as credible witnesses to our own experiences," as Vonny LeClerc, one of his interviewees, puts it.[16] Yong adds that this is "especially common when women have subjective symptoms like pain or fatigue, as most long-haulers do."[17] Medical racism also plays a significant part in denying a patient's epistemic authority about their experiences of their body and illness. Lindsey Sitz's video documentary created for the *Washington Post* records and amplifies Cynthia Adinig's story of long Covid and medical gaslighting, a story Adinig herself had first documented on social media as a means of connecting with others about their shared experiences of long Covid. Like Callard and Perego, Adinig has contributed to making long Covid, and she identifies herself on her website as a

14. Callard and Perego, "How and Why Patients Made Long Covid," 4.

15. Yong, "COVID-19 Can Last for Several Months."

16. Yong.

17. Yong. In my book *Treatments,* I conclude by discussing how pain and suffering create a *différend* for medicine: that is, following Lyotard's use of the term, an incommensurability between the doctor and patient in the doctor–patient relationship, 149. I argue that despite, or indeed because of, this incommensurability, an ethical imperative—what I called an "ethics of failure"—can be the beginning of searching for new forms of engagement, both aesthetic and political, 150.

"long Covid patient and advocate" who recently gave testimony to Congress on the coronavirus crisis.[18]

The text included with the video on the *Washington Post* website summarizes Adinig's harrowing story as follows:

> Over the last eight months, 35-year-old Cynthia Adinig has been to the hospital upwards of 20 times for debilitating symptoms related to long-haul covid-19, ranging from heart palpitations to severe malnutrition. On some visits, Adinig feared for her life, but was pushed out of the hospital before she felt ready to leave. With few answers from doctors, Adinig turned to an online support group for connection and understanding.[19]

It is a familiar narrative of a confounding illness, dismissiveness and disbelief from doctors and other health practitioners, and eventually finding support from fellow sufferers on social media. It is also clearly a story of medical racism, as we witness Adinig filming her visits to the hospital on her phone and posting footage on Twitter of hospital staff neglecting her and hospital security forcing her to leave for supposedly being disruptive even as she is suffering and weak from "heart palpitations, low oxygen levels, dehydration, and severe malnutrition."

Sitz's film begins by showing Adinig on September 27, 2020, moving slowly outside her apartment building, as she assesses her current condition: "Feeling okay today. For now. It's like an hour-by-hour kind of thing." Adinig then describes how she, her husband, and their four-year-old son all got sick in March 2020. The voice-over explains, "It was a mild sickness—scratchy throat, no cough, low-grade fever," and we learn from Adinig that they were never tested for Covid because of strict testing requirements at the time. Adinig, however, does not recover. Instead, she describes the onset of a persistent and debilitating condition, which arrived on Mother's

18. "Cynthia Adinig Gives Testimony on the Coronavirus Crisis," August 2, 2022, https://www.youtube.com/watch?v=cn6y15ZjyLo&t=2s.

19. Sitz, "Why This Black Woman with 'Long Covid' Feels the Medical Community Has Failed Her."

Day—March 10, 2020, after Adinig's husband treated her to one of her favorite foods, shrimp. Along with interviews with Adinig and others, footage of her with her family, and film she took with her phone while at the hospital, the film also includes animated sequences created by animator Daron Taylor. Thus, as Adinig recalls her Mother's Day treat and her experience after eating the shrimp, we see her cartoon avatar with her hands holding her stomach and chest, as she says, "I just started feeling weird." As Adinig describes her symptoms ("Like, my jaw felt really tight, and my heart just felt like it was racing. My eyes got blurry."), the animation visually captures the overwhelming, dizzying feeling of suddenly becoming sick. Jagged forms enter the film frame, invading Adinig's cartoon avatar's space as her figure wobbles and her clothing and skin coloring change from bright and healthy-looking to drab and washed-out variations of gray. A pale peach blob pulsates from her heart, ripples expanding outward, as the symptoms take over her body. The animation creates a visual reenactment of becoming sick—subjective symptoms of pain and bodily discomfort are rendered via what we might describe as a graphic phenomenological vocabulary of illness. Adinig's symptoms are animated into a visual language that is disturbing yet relatable.

The film also documents Adinig's activity on social media as she shares her own experiences of illness and mistreatment. For example, we see a screen grab of a Twitter post from May 26, 2020, in which Adinig tweets "In the ER for the 3rd time with heart palpitations please pray" along with a selfie of her in a mask in a hospital examination room. The film's voiceover states, "Without answers from the medical community, long haulers have turned to each other for support." We then see a supportive exchange between Adinig and Miranda Erlanson in a Facebook group for Covid long-haulers. Adinig posts, on September 8, 2020, that she is "So thankful for my fellow post covid friends. Couldn't ask for kinder, stronger, more resourceful or more giving group to suffer through this with #longhauler," and Erlanson responds, "Right back at ya! [three heart emojis]," followed by a humorous exchange about "wheelchair decor." This sequence showing the importance of social media for creating networks of support is then followed by conversations between the two women on Zoom, presumably made for the film. They recall how they became aware of each other on social media because they shared similar symptoms, especially difficulty eating and even drinking water. In their Zoom conversation, Adinig says to Erlanson that, seeing posts from Erlanson, she thought, "Oh, she's my COVID twin" (Figure 6). The Zoom gallery format is ideal for capturing this statement about their feeling of close connection that emerges from their similarly bizarre and debilitating symptoms. The film's voiceover notes that, "Both women have struggled to find doctors who take them seriously," and Adinig jokes of a typical doctor's response to her and her condition: "Oh, it's a hysterical woman. I need to give her an anti-depressant." Here again, hysteria becomes the default diagnostic category for

Figure 6. Cynthia Adinig and Miranda Erlanson recall how they became aware of each other on social media because they shared similar symptoms, especially difficulty eating and even drinking water. In their Zoom conversation, Adinig says to Erlanson that, seeing posts from Erlanson, she thought, "Oh, she's my COVID twin." Screen grab from Lindsey Sitz, "Why This Black Woman with 'Long Covid' Feels the Medical Community Has Failed Her," *The Washington Post*, February 2, 2021. https://www.washingtonpost.com/video/topics/coronavirus/why-this-black -woman-with-long-covid-feels-the-medical-community-has-failed-her/2021/02 /02/68ce212c-f1ba-4983-8d07-d2fd5e8e4429_video.html.

an illness not yet fully understood biologically, and the means by which doctors dismiss the epistemic authority of long-haulers like Adinig and Erlanson on their experiences of their bodies.

Despite their similar symptomatology and identification with each other through shared symptoms and mutual support, Adinig's and Erlanson's experiences with health care are quite different, which Erlanson realizes can only be explained by the fact that Erlanson is white and Adinig is Black. Adinig describes being treated "as a threat" by hospital staff even though she is usually in a wheelchair. She documents on social media how one hospital, Inova Alexandria, called security on her rather than helping her. And Adinig is shocked to learn that she was drug tested on numerous visits to the ER, even though she has no history whatsoever of drug use. Erlanson is also shocked to learn Adinig has been drug tested. She tells Adinig on Zoom, "I saw your video and I really felt like there's nothing different between us except our skin color. Why are they treating you like that? Didn't you tell me that they keep drug-testing you? I've never been drug-tested." Sitz interviews Iameta Nicole Barlow, a community health psychologist, on medical racism. Barlow states, "Institutions aren't always safe for marginalized people, particularly Black people." She describes how Black women are often viewed as "having an attitude" if they advocate for themselves, as Adinig tries to do. Sitz contacts Inova Alexandria for a statement and they refuse to take responsibility for their actions, saying, in a classic apology-that-doesn't-apologize, "we are sorry to hear that this patient was dissatisfied with her experience."[20] The film ends with some positive signs that Adinig's health is improving slowly. But it also ends with this brutal realization from Adinig regarding racism and illness politics in the United States: "You have to come to grips with there is no safe space for Black people in America." This is a stark reminder for all of us of how illness politics intersects

20. For more on the apology as speech act, see Sara Ahmed, *The Cultural Politics of Emotion* (New York: Routledge, 2004).

with racial, sexual, and class politics. This realization, however, does not end Adinig's illness politics; rather it spurs her on in an ongoing struggle happening now in multiple modalities. This ongoing struggle in the present points toward other possible futures beyond denialism and dismissiveness to new forms of illness and disability politics in action.

I end with an image of long Covid as both an illness and illness politics characterized by ongoingness. Like #ADAPTandRESIST, #LongCOVID and the illness politics surrounding the making of it make visible what might otherwise remain hidden from public attention. And as with #CripTheVote and #TimeForUnrest, online community building creates the conditions of possibility for participation of people otherwise missing from public life. These hashtags provide snapshots of illness and disability in action in the present moment, and through the hashtags, the violence and exclusions of recent policies are revealed. These hashtags also reveal a multiplicity of practices—of vulnerability and heroism, confrontation and compromise, exhaustion and endurance—in the ongoing struggle for care, access, and participation in public life.

Acknowledgments

In all my work, I have sought to think illness and politics together. This has been a conceptual and formal challenge. As part of the University of Minnesota Press's Forerunners series, which publishes shorter books of "thought-in-process scholarship, where intense analysis, questioning, and speculation take the lead," *Illness Politics and Hashtag Activism* continues this work. This shorter, more accessible format was nonetheless a long time coming. Many people and places helped me do this work, and I am grateful for numerous collaborations and provocations over the years.

I first presented material that would eventually become this book at the Artificial Life: Debating Medical Modernity symposium at UC Riverside. I thank Juliet McMullin for the invitation and camaraderie over the years. More recently, I presented some of this work as part of the Conceptualizing Vulnerability Zoom roundtable organized by Pramod K. Nayar, who is the UNESCO Chair in Vulnerability Studies at the University of Hyderabad. I am also grateful to Lisa Käll and Kristin Zeiler at Stockholm University and Nythamar de Oliveira at Pontifical Catholic University, Porto Alegre, Brazil, for invitations to present related work.

Many intellectual spaces have been generative for my thinking, including the online medical history blog *Nursing Clio,* which published an early version of chapter 2. Thanks especially to editors Laura Ansley and Jacqueline Antonovich for their encouragement and enthusiasm. I also published an early version of chapter 5 as part of a Front Matter section on the topic of protest for *Literature & Medicine*. That journal has long been a source of support for my work, and I especially want to thank editor Michael Blackie and managing editor Anna Fenton-Hathaway for their vision and care. It has been a pleasure to serve on the editorial board of *Literature & Medicine* for many years with so many amazing colleagues, including Catherine Belling, Tod Chambers, Rita Charon, Sayantani DasGupta, Rebecca Garden, Anne Hudson Jones, Ann Jurecic, Travis Chi Wing Lau, Thomas Long, Juliet McMullin, Kirsten Ostherr, Lorenzo Servitje, Maura Spiegel, Susan Squier, Martha Stoddard Holmes, Jaipreet Virdi, and Priscilla Wald.

At Stony Brook, collaborating with Nancy Tomes, Karen Lloyd, Andy Flescher, and Susan Scheckel on the Critical Health Studies/ Pandemic Narratives project has been a source of pleasure amid the harsh realities of the pandemic. It is with great sadness that I remember my dear colleague and friend Adrián Pérez-Melgosa, who in both his work and life modeled practices of healing and resiliency.

I have had the great good fortune to work with Leah Pennywark at University of Minnesota Press on this project. I am so grateful for her enthusiastic and generous support and guidance throughout this process. As always, Anne Carter has been a calming force through the production process. And thanks to Mike Stoffel for his careful copy editing.

Thank you to the anonymous reader who offered thoughtful comments, especially in understanding that the turn from electoral politics to sick and disabled activism is the heart of this project, which seeks to showcase the multiple spaces and temporalities of illness and disability politics. I am grateful to and awed by sick and disabled activists doing political work in a variety of ways. I want to give a special shout out to Alice Wong, who is a force on social media—smart and incisive in her critiques of ableism and warm and welcoming in her creation of online community for disabled people and their allies. She may be the best coiner of hashtags I know. One of my favorites is #SuckItAbleism, a hashtag she started to point to the absurdity of plastic straw bans to stem the tide of climate change. I also thank Alice and artist Micah Bazant for permission to reproduce the Crip the Vote image Bazant created in collaboration with Alice.

As this book was going to press, new stories about illness politics kept arising. Although I engage briefly with the illness politics surrounding John Fetterman's successful run for election to the U.S. Senate, I was not able to give that story the attention it deserves. Yet, the stories and images keep coming. We see Senator Fetterman choke up in a hearing with disability activists when he showed how his phone's transcription tool helps him to communicate with others. GIFs of Mitch McConnell freezing up during press conferences have circulated widely on social media. And Robert F. Kennedy Jr.'s presidential campaign seems based primarily on an ableist illness politics. Not to mention the *New Yorker*'s October 2 cover by cartoonist Barry Blitt, "The Race for Office," showing Trump, McConnell, Nancy Pelosi, and Joe Biden using walkers to compete in a road race. I mention these here and now to suggest both the timeliness and ongoingness of this project, and to encourage further investigations and conversations into how illness politics operates in the present.

I am grateful for the unwavering support of my family. My dad and his partner Shirl Pessl, ever curious and creative. My brilliant sisters, Andrea Diedrich Kumar and Dawn Diedrich, and their partners, Vikram Kumar and Joe Foley. My amazing niblings, Nikhil and Sona Kumar and Jack Boyette, instill hope for a bright future. In memory of my mother, Fran Diedrich, who was steadfast not showy in her support of me and my sisters.

In this book, as with illness, ongoingness both happens to us and is something we do that opens new possibilities and ways of life. As always, I am indebted to Victoria Hesford for reminding me of the pleasures and possibilities of ongoingness. As I was finishing the book, we had to say goodbye to our best pup Cyril, who trained us to play and love better for thirteen years. A month after we adopted him, he was diagnosed with Addison's disease, which is a chronic but treatable condition. After Cyril's diagnosis, I began reading about Addison's, including about how John F. Kennedy kept his diagnosis of the illness secret in the 1960 presidential election. Thus, in many ways, our experience with Cyril's Addison's was the beginning of this book on illness politics.

(Continued from page iii)

Forerunners: Ideas First

Aaron Jaffe
Spoiler Alert: A Critical Guide

Don Ihde
Medical Technics

Jonathan Beecher Field
Town Hall Meetings and the Death of Deliberation

Jennifer Gabrys
How to Do Things with Sensors

Naa Oyo A. Kwate
**Burgers in Blackface: Anti-Black Restaurants
Then and Now**

Arne De Boever
Against Aesthetic Exceptionalism

Steve Mentz
Break Up the Anthropocene

John Protevi
Edges of the State

Matthew J. Wolf-Meyer
**Theory for the World to Come: Speculative Fiction and
Apocalyptic Anthropology**

Nicholas Tampio
Learning versus the Common Core

Kathryn Yusoff
A Billion Black Anthropocenes or None

Kenneth J. Saltman
The Swindle of Innovative Educational Finance

Ginger Nolan
The Neocolonialism of the Global Village

Joanna Zylinska
The End of Man: A Feminist Counterapocalypse

Robert Rosenberger
Callous Objects: Designs against the Homeless

William E. Connolly
**Aspirational Fascism: The Struggle for Multifaceted
Democracy under Trumpism**

Lisa Diedrich is professor of Women's, Gender, and Sexuality Studies at Stony Brook University. She is the author of *Indirect Action: Schizophrenia, Epilepsy, AIDS, and the Course of Health Activism* and *Treatments: Language, Politics, and the Culture of Illness.*